Busy Ant Maths

2nd EDITION

Textbook 4

T0312332

Series editor and author: Peter Clarke

William Collins' dream of knowledge for all began with the publication of his first book in 1819.

A self-educated mill worker, he not only enriched millions of lives, but also founded a flourishing publishing house. Today, staying true to this spirit, Collins books are packed with inspiration, innovation and practical expertise.

They place you at the centre of a world of possibility and give you exactly what you need to explore it.

Collins. Freedom to teach.

Published by Collins

An imprint of HarperCollins*Publishers*
The News Building, 1 London Bridge Street, London, SE1 9GF, UK

HarperCollins*Publishers*
Macken House, 39/40 Mayor Street Upper, Dublin 1, D01 C9W8, Ireland

Browse the complete Collins catalogue at
collins.co.uk

10 9 8 7 6 5 4 3 2 1

ISBN 978-0-00-861375-4

British Library Cataloguing-in-Publication Data

A catalogue record for this publication is available from the British Library.

Series editor: Peter Clarke
Author: Peter Clarke
Product manager: Holly Woolnough
Editorial assistant: Nalisha Vansia
Copy editor: Tanya Solomons
Proofreader: Catherine Dakin
Illustrator: Ann Paganuzzi
Cover designer: Amparo Barrera
Cover illustrator: Amparo Barrera
Internal designer: 2Hoots Publishing Services
Typesetter: David Jimenez
Production controller: Alhady Ali
Printed and bound in Great Britain by Martins the Printers

Busy Ant Maths 2nd edition components are compatible with the 1st edition of Busy Ant Maths.

This book is produced from independently certified FSC™ paper to ensure responsible forest management.

For more information visit: harpercollins.co.uk/green

Acknowledgements

p42t FARBAI/Shutterstock; p42c White Space Illustrations/Shutterstock; p60 Michiru13/Shutterstock.

Contents

Multiplication and division

Fractions

Decimals

Year 4 Number facts

How to use this book

This book shows different pictures, models and images (representations) to explain important mathematical ideas to do with number.

The key words related to the mathematical ideas are shown in **colour**. It's important that you understand what each of these words mean.

At the start of each double page is a brief description of the key mathematical ideas.

The main part of each double page explains the mathematical ideas. It might include pictures, models or an example.

Your teacher will talk to you about the images on the pages.

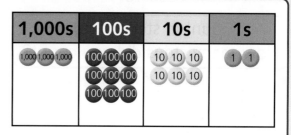

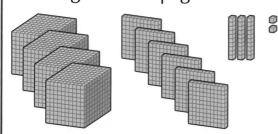

1,000s	100s	10s	1s
1,000 1,000 1,000	100 100 100 100 100 100 100 100 100	10 10 10 10 10 10	1 1

×	30	4
2	10 10 10 10 10 10	1 1 1 1 1 1 1 1

60　+　8　=　68

Sometimes there might be questions to think about or an activity to do.

 Say

 Build

 Draw

 Write

Pages 6–7

This refers to mathematical ideas on other pages that you need to understand before learning about the ideas on these two pages.

Pages 24–29, 48–55

This refers to mathematical ideas on other pages that use or build upon the ideas on these two pages.

 This helps you think more deeply about the mathematical ideas.

 Hint　Use the pages in this book to help you answer the questions in the Pupil Books.

Represent numbers to 10,000

Four-digit numbers are made of thousands (1,000s), hundreds (100s), tens (10s) and ones (1s). The place of each digit in a number tells us its value. Composing and decomposing numbers to 10,000 into thousands, hundreds, tens and ones makes them easier to calculate.

Look at the Base 10.

Count in steps of 10.
How many steps did you count?

Count in steps of 100.
How many steps did you count?

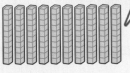

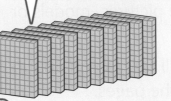

We can also say that:

10 **tens** are **equivalent** to 1 **hundred**.

10 **hundreds** are equivalent to 1 thousand. We write 1 thousand as 1,000.

1 thousand 1,000

= 1,000 ones 1

= 100 tens 10

= 10 **hundreds** 100

A **4-digit number** can be written with a comma or a space separating the **hundreds** and the thousands (4,632 or 4 632). You might also see 4-digit numbers written without a comma or a space (4632).

Look at the Gattegno chart below. It shows ones, tens, **hundreds** and thousands.

What patterns do you notice?

How are the rows the same? How are they different?

What happens in each column of numbers?

Say

Point to a number in the thousands, **hundreds**, tens and ones rows.
Say your number in different ways.

There are
4 thousands,
6 **hundreds**,
3 tens and
2 ones in 4,632.

4,632 **is equal to** 4,000 **add** 600 add 30 add 2.

1,000	2,000	3,000	4,000	5,000	6,000	7,000	8,000	9,000
100	200	300	400	500	600	700	800	900
10	20	30	40	50	60	70	80	90
1	2	3	4	5	6	7	8	9

We can use different objects, pictures and models to **compose** and **decompose** 4-digit numbers into thousands, **hundreds**, tens and ones and show the **place value** of each **digit**.

To compose a number, we use our knowledge of place value to **create** a number, for example: 4,000 + 600 + 30 + 2 = 4,632

To decompose a number, we use our knowledge of place value to **separate** or **partition** a number, for example: 4,632 = 4,000 + 600 + 30 + 2

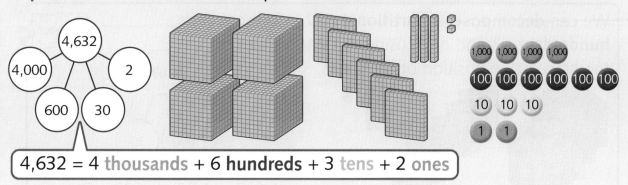

4,632 = 4 thousands + 6 **hundreds** + 3 tens + 2 ones

Look at this place value chart. To find the **value** of each digit we look at its position in the chart.

The digit 4 is in the thousands position. The value of the 4 is 4 thousands or 4,000.

The digit 2 is in the ones position. The value of the 2 is 2 ones or 2.

1,000s	100s	10s	1s
4	6	3	2

The digit 6 is in the **hundreds** position. The value of the 6 is 6 **hundreds** or 600.

The digit 3 is in the tens position. The value of the 3 is 3 tens or 30.

To find the whole number, we add the values together.

4,000 + 600 + 30 + 2 = 4,632

What numbers have been decomposed to show their place value?

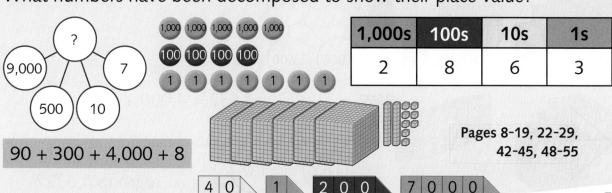

90 + 300 + 4,000 + 8

Pages 8-19, 22-29, 42-45, 48-55

7

Represent numbers to 10,000 in different ways

Pages 6-7

We can decompose numbers to 10,000 into thousands, hundreds, tens and ones to show the place value of each digit. We can also decompose (or regroup) 4-digit numbers in other ways.

We can **decompose** or **partition** 4,632 into thousands, hundreds, tens and ones using our knowledge of the place value position of the digits.

Remember

4,632
4,000   2
600   30

$$4,632 = 4,000 + 600 + 30 + 2$$

Numbers can also be decomposed or **regrouped** in other ways to help with calculations.

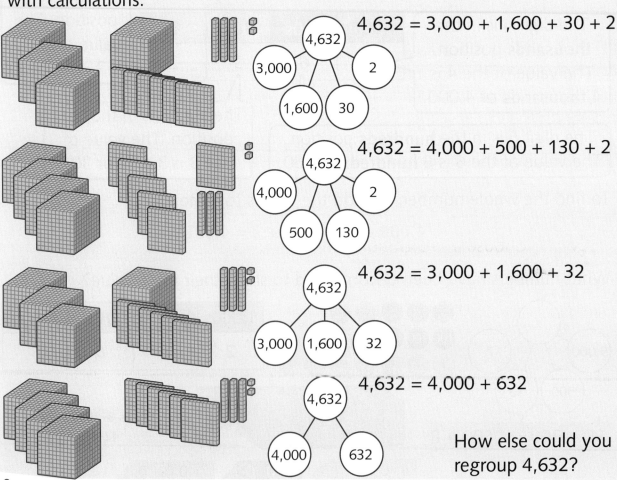

$$4,632 = 3,000 + 1,600 + 30 + 2$$

4,632
3,000   2
1,600   30

$$4,632 = 4,000 + 500 + 130 + 2$$

4,632
4,000   2
500   130

$$4,632 = 3,000 + 1,600 + 32$$

4,632
3,000   1,600   32

$$4,632 = 4,000 + 632$$

4,632
4,000   632

How else could you regroup 4,632?

We can decompose 3,857 into thousands, **hundreds**, tens and ones.

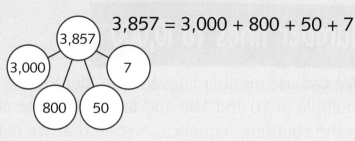

$$3,857 = 3,000 + 800 + 50 + 7$$

We can regroup 3,857 in other ways.

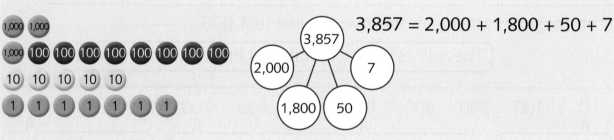

$$3,857 = 2,000 + 1,800 + 50 + 7$$

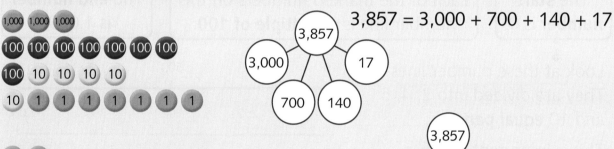

$$3,857 = 3,000 + 700 + 140 + 17$$

$$3,857 = 2,000 + 1,700 + 157$$

Can you think of other ways to regroup 3,857?

1,000 to 9,999

Choose a 4-digit number.

How many different ways can you regroup your number?

Build

What objects could you use?

Draw

What pictures or models might you draw?

Write

How would you write your number as an addition calculation?

Pages 24-29, 48-55

9

Number lines to 10,000

Pages 6-7

We can use number lines to help identify the previous and next multiple of 10 and 100 and to estimate the position of numbers in the counting sequence. A scale that we read and interpret on a measuring instrument or a graph is also a type of number line.

Let's begin by looking at this number line to 1,000.

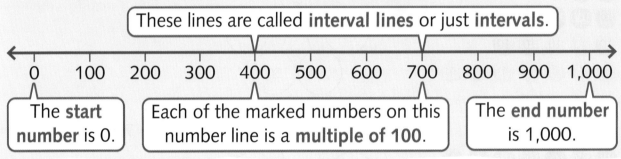

These lines are called **interval lines** or just **intervals**.

| 0 | 100 | 200 | 300 | 400 | 500 | 600 | 700 | 800 | 900 | 1,000 |

The **start number** is 0.

Each of the marked numbers on this number line is a **multiple of 100**.

The **end number** is 1,000.

Look at these number lines. They are divided into 2, 4, 5 and 10 **equal parts**.

This is important because these are the intervals commonly found on measuring instruments and graph scales.

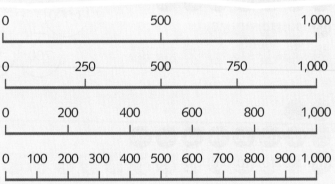

Count on and **back** in **steps of** 500, 250, 200 and 100 from 0 to 1,000 and beyond.

Now look at this number line.

How is it the same as the number lines above? How is it different?

Each of the marked numbers on this number line is a **multiple of 1,000**.

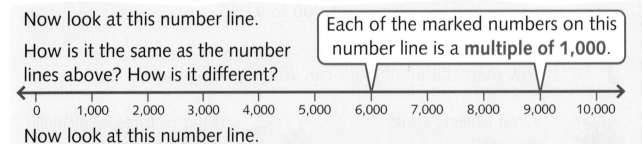

| 0 | 1,000 | 2,000 | 3,000 | 4,000 | 5,000 | 6,000 | 7,000 | 8,000 | 9,000 | 10,000 |

Now look at this number line.

How is it the same as the number line above? How is it different?

What numbers do the **unmarked intervals** stand for?

| 0 | 1,000 | 2,000 | 3,000 | 4,000 | 5,000 | 6,000 | 7,000 | 8,000 | 9,000 | 10,000 |

Count on and **back** in **steps of 1,000** from 0 to 10,000.

Look carefully at the start and end numbers on these number lines.

What number is each of the arrows pointing to?

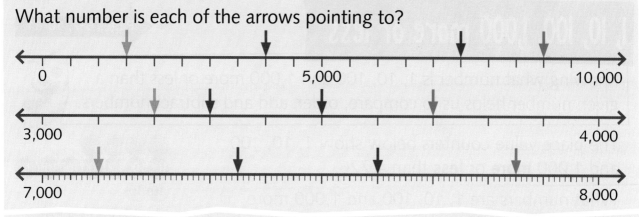

Which multiples of 1,000 do each of these numbers come before and after?

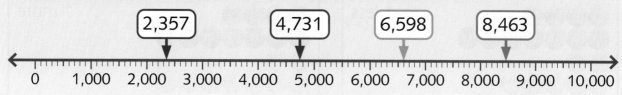

Look carefully at the start and end numbers on these number lines.

The numbers marked below the number lines, such as 5,400 and 8,700 are 4-digit multiples of 100.

Which 4-digit multiples of 100 do each of these numbers come before and after?

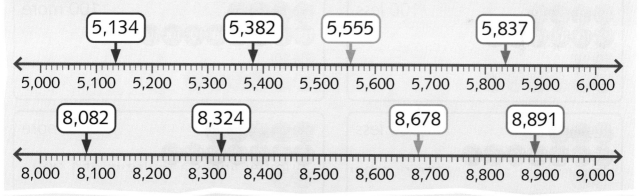

Estimate the number each arrow is pointing to.

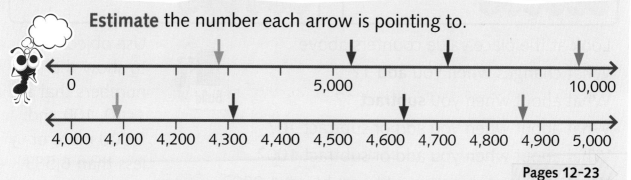

Pages 12–23

1, 10, 100, 1,000 more or less

Pages 6-7, 10-11

Knowing what number is 1, 10, 100 and 1,000 more or less than a given number helps us to compare, order, add and subtract numbers.

The place value counters below show 1, 10, 100 and 1,000 **more** or **less** than 4,726.

What numbers are 1, 10, 100 and 1,000 more or less than 4,726?

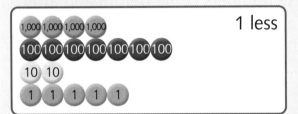
1 less

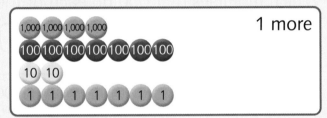
1 more

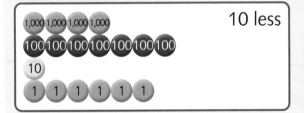
10 less

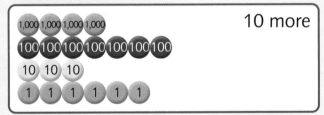
10 more

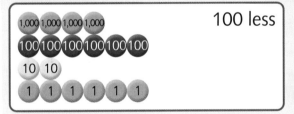
100 less

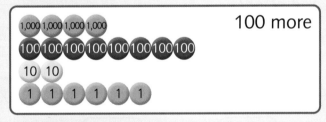
100 more

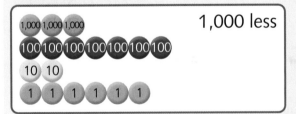
1,000 less

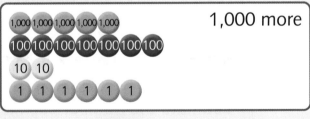
1,000 more

Look at the place value counters above.

What changes when you **add** 1?

What about when you **subtract** 1?

What about when you add or subtract 10?

What about when you add or subtract 100?

What changes when you add or subtract 1,000?

Build

Use objects to show the numbers that are 1, 10, 100 and 1,000 more or less than 6,583.

When finding 1, 10 and 100 more or less of some numbers, we cross a **multiple** of 10, 100 or 1,000, and we need to make an **exchange**.

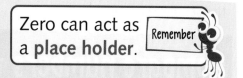
Zero can act as a **place holder**. Remember

In these examples, which columns change? Which stay the same?

100 more than 3,962 is 4,062.

1,000s	100s	10s	1s
1,000 1,000 1,000	100 100 100 100 100 100 100 100 100	10 10 10 10 10 10	1 1

 100 more

1,000s	100s	10s	1s
1,000 1,000 1,000 1,000	100 100 100 100 100 100 100 100 100 100	10 10 10 10 10 10	1 1

10 more than 2,996 is 3,006.

1,000s	100s	10s	1s
1,000 1,000	100 100 100 100 100 100 100 100 100	10 10 10 10 10 10 10 10 10	1 1 1 1 1 1

 10 more

1,000s	100s	10s	1s
1,000 1,000 1,000	100 100 100 100 100 100 100 100 100 100	10 10 10 10 10 10 10 10 10 10	1 1 1 1 1 1

100 less than 5,074 is 4,974.

1,000s	100s	10s	1s
1,000 1,000 1,000 1,000 1,000		10 10 10 10 10 10 10	1 1 1 1

 100 less

1,000s	100s	10s	1s
1,000 1,000 1,000 1,000 1,000	100 100 100 100 100 100 100 100 100 100	10 10 10 10 10 10 10	1 1 1 1

10 less than 4,608 is 4,598.

1,000s	100s	10s	1s
1,000 1,000 1,000 1,000	100 100 100 100 100 100		1 1 1 1 1 1 1 1

10 less

1,000s	100s	10s	1s
1,000 1,000 1,000 1,000	100 100 100 100 100 100	10 10 10 10 10 10 10 10 10	1 1 1 1 1 1 1 1

Look at these number cards.

What is 1, 10, 100 and 1,000 more than each number?

What is 1, 10, 100 and 1,000 less than each number?

Which numbers were easy to find?

Which were more difficult? Why was this?

4,999	6,998

2,048	3,901

3,648

Pages 14-15, 24-29

Compare numbers to 10,000

Pages 6-7, 10-11

When we compare numbers, we use language such as greater/smaller than and more/less than, and the inequality symbols > and <.

It's important to remember what the **inequality** symbols mean.

greater than | less than

> | <

When we **compare** numbers, it's important to start with the **digits** with the greatest **place value**. If the digits with the greatest place value are the same, we look at the place value columns to the right until they are different digits.

When comparing 4-digit numbers, start by looking at the **thousands** digits.

4,712 has 4 thousands. ▷ 4,**712**

3,523 has 3 thousands. ▷ 3,**523**

4,712 is greater than 3,523.

3,523 is less than 4,712.

4,712 > 3,523

3,523 < 4,712

If the **thousands** digits are the same, look at the **hundreds** digits.

2,631 has 6 **hundreds**. ▷ 2,**631**

2,854 has 8 **hundreds**. ▷ 2,**854**

2,631 is less than 2,854.

2,854 is greater than 2,631.

2,631 < 2,854

2,854 > 2,631

If the **thousands** and **hundreds** digits are the same, look at the **tens** digits.

7,235 has 3 tens. ▷ 7,2**3**5

7,269 has 6 tens. ▷ 7,2**6**9

7,235 is less than 7,269.

7,269 is greater than 7,235.

7,235 < 7,269

7,269 > 7,235

If the **thousands**, **hundreds** and **tens** digits are the same, look at the **ones** digits.

5,376 has 6 ones. ▷ 5,37**6**

5,374 has 4 ones. ▷ 5,37**4**

5,376 is greater than 5,374.

5,374 is less than 5,376.

5,376 > 5,374

5,374 < 5,376

Which is the greater number in each pair?

Should you start by comparing the thousands, **hundreds**, tens or ones first? Why?

four thousand, two hundred and fifty-six   4,756

5,000 + 200 + 40 + 3   1 + 20 + 5,000 + 300

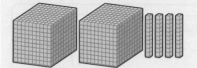   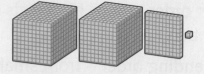

8,354   8,345

42 hundreds   40 hundreds and 20 tens

 Write each pair of numbers above as 4-digit numbers.

Use the <, > and = symbols to compare each pair of numbers.

We can also use a number line to help compare numbers.

 Say What statements can you make comparing pairs of marked numbers on these number lines?

 Write Write these statements using the < and > symbols.

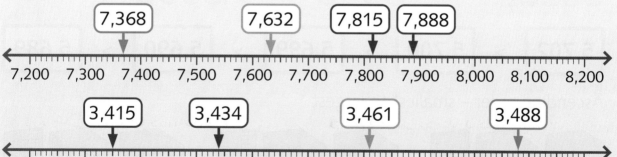

What numbers could go in the boxes?

 Write 3,000 + 800 + 2 + 50 < ☐   ☐ < 28 hundreds

☐ > 1,000 1,000 1,000 1,000 10 10 1 1 1

two thousand, nine hundred and one > ☐   **Pages 16–17, 74–75**

15

Order numbers to 10,000

Pages 6-7, 10-11, 14-15

Numbers can be ordered from smallest to largest/greatest or from largest/greatest to smallest. We can also use the inequality symbols < and > when ordering numbers.

We can **order** groups of objects or a set of numbers:

in **ascending** order – from **smallest** to **largest/greatest**

or in **descending** order – from largest/greatest to smallest.

When we order numbers, it's important to start with the **digits** with the greatest **place value**. If the digits with the greatest place value are the same, we look at the place value columns to the right until they are different digits.

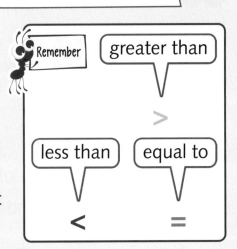

Remember

greater than

>

less than   equal to

<   =

Descending order – largest to smallest

5,702 > 5,700 > 5,699 > 5,690 > 5,689

Ascending order – smallest to largest

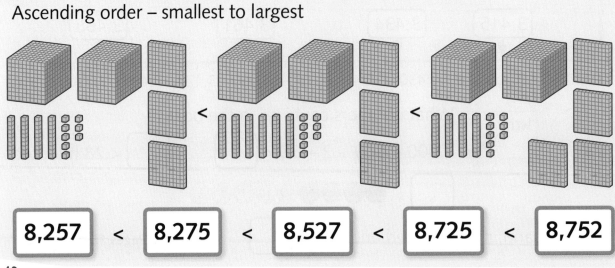

8,257 < 8,275 < 8,527 < 8,725 < 8,752

Look at this set of numbers.

What's the same about each number?

What's different?

| 3,630 | 3,360 | 3,306 |
| 3,036 | 3,603 | |

Which digits are the most important ones to consider when ordering a set of 4-digit numbers? Why is this?

When ordering 4-digit numbers, if the **thousands** digits are equal in **value**, what do you look at next?

Write Write the set of numbers above in ascending order.

[ ] < [ ] < [ ] < [ ] < [ ]

Now write the numbers in descending order.

[ ] > [ ] > [ ] > [ ] > [ ]

What do you notice? Why is this?

We can also use a number line to help order numbers.

| 8,259 | 8,278 | 8,251 | 8,271 | 8,215 |

8,215   8,251 8,259 8,271 8,278

8,200 8,210 8,220 8,230 8,240 8,250 8,260 8,270 8,280 8,290 8,300

Write Use the 4,450 to 4,550 number line below to order each set of numbers. Start with the smallest number.

| 4,516 | 4,536 | 4,546 | | 4,487 | 4,548 | 4,508 |
| | 4,461 | 4,453 | | | 4,458 | 4,478 |

4,450 4,460 4,470 4,480 4,490 4,500 4,510 4,520 4,530 4,540 4,550

[ ] < [ ] < [ ] < [ ] < [ ]

Pages 74-75

Round numbers to the nearest 10, 100 or 1,000

Pages 6–7, 10–11

Rounding means changing a number to another number that is close to it in value. Rounding numbers often makes them easier to use. It's a useful strategy to use when estimating.

Round to the nearest 10

We **round** 2-digit numbers **up** or **down**, depending on which **multiple of 10** a number is closer to. A number line is a useful tool to help with rounding.

> 32 is closer to 30 than to 40 so we **round down** to the **previous** multiple of 10, which is 30.

> 37 is closer to 40 than to 30 so we **round up** to the **next** multiple of 10, which is 40.

30   31   32   33   34   35   36   37   38   39   40

> Look at the number 35. It's exactly **halfway between** 30 and 40. The rule is to round up a number with 5 **ones** to the next multiple of 10.

To round numbers to the nearest multiple of 10, look at the ones **digit** to decide whether to round up to the next multiple of 10 or round down to the previous multiple of 10.

We can round 3-digit numbers to the nearest multiple of 10.

> 463 rounds down to 460.   465 rounds up to 470.   466 rounds up to 470.

460   461   462   463   464   465   466   467   468   469   470

We can also round 4-digit numbers to the nearest multiple of 10.

> 3,524 rounds down to 3,520.   3,525 rounds up to 3,530.

3,520 3,521 3,522 3,523 3,524 3,525 3,526 3,527 3,528 3,529 3,530

> 3,528 rounds up to 3,530.

Write Round each of these numbers to the nearest 10.

| 842 | 56 | 2,804 | 368 | 7,365 | 19 |

Round to the nearest 100

We can round 3- and 4-digit numbers to the nearest **multiple of 100**.

To round to the nearest multiple of 100, look at the tens digit to decide whether to round up to the next multiple of 100 or round down to the previous multiple of 100.

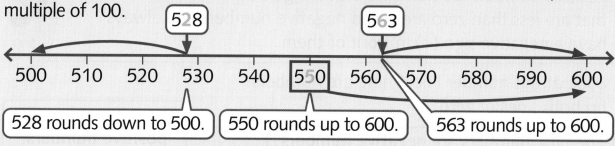

528 rounds down to 500. 550 rounds up to 600. 563 rounds up to 600.

We can also round 4-digit numbers to the nearest multiple of 100.

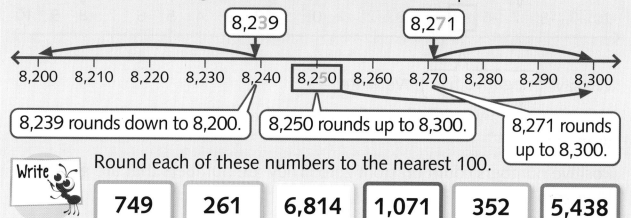

8,239 rounds down to 8,200. 8,250 rounds up to 8,300. 8,271 rounds up to 8,300.

Write Round each of these numbers to the nearest 100.

| 749 | 261 | 6,814 | 1,071 | 352 | 5,438 |

Round to the nearest 1,000

We can round 4-digit numbers to the nearest **multiple of 1,000**.

To round to the nearest multiple of 1,000, look at the **hundreds** digit to decide whether to round up to the next multiple of 1,000 or round down to the previous multiple of 1,000.

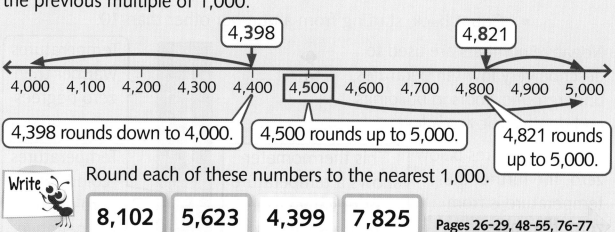

4,398 rounds down to 4,000. 4,500 rounds up to 5,000. 4,821 rounds up to 5,000.

Write Round each of these numbers to the nearest 1,000.

| 8,102 | 5,623 | 4,399 | 7,825 |

Pages 26-29, 48-55, 76-77

Negative numbers

Pages 10–11

Positive numbers are numbers that are greater than zero. Numbers that are less than zero are called negative numbers and always have a negative sign (–) in front of them.

Look at this number line. There are numbers on both sides of **zero**.

The red numbers are **positive numbers**.

The blue numbers are **negative numbers**.

–10 –9 –8 –7 –6 –5 –4 –3 –2 –1 0 1 2 3 4 5 6 7 8 9 10

We say: negative five   We write: –5

Negative numbers count back from zero. They are numbers that are **less than zero**.

Positive numbers count on from zero. They are numbers that are **greater than zero**.

Zero is neither a positive nor a negative number. It's the separation point between positive and negative numbers.

Say   Look at the number line above.

- Count on from –10 to 10.
- Count back from 10 to –10.
- Count on, starting from a number other than –10.
- Count back, starting from a number other than 10.

Negative numbers are used to describe very low temperatures, underground floors in buildings and depths below sea level.

For temperatures below zero, the further the temperature is from zero, the colder it is.

This thermometer shows a temperature of negative four degrees Celsius.

Temperatures warmer than zero degrees are positive.

Temperatures colder than zero degrees are negative.

°C
5
4
3
2
1
0
1
2
3
4
5

For floors below zero, the further the floor is from the ground floor, the deeper the floor is underground.

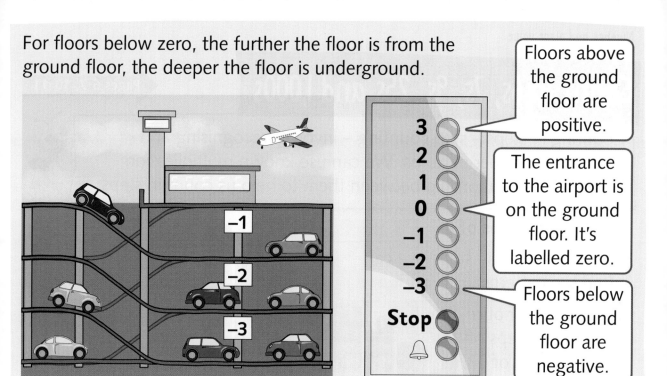

Floors above the ground floor are positive.

The entrance to the airport is on the ground floor. It's labelled zero.

Floors below the ground floor are negative.

The submarine travelled 100 metres below zero (sea level).

It then travelled a further 200 metres down to sit on the ocean floor.

What is the depth of the submarine below sea level?

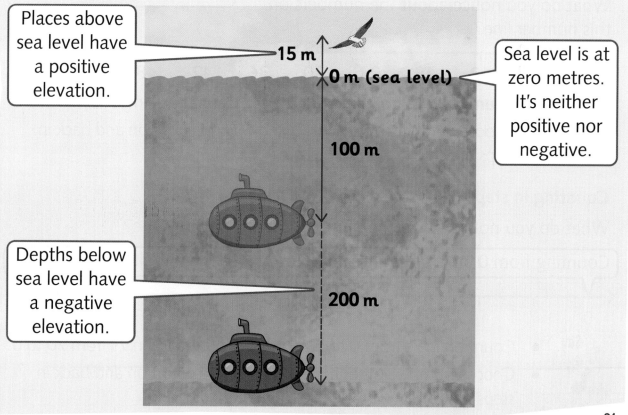

Places above sea level have a positive elevation.

Sea level is at zero metres. It's neither positive nor negative.

Depths below sea level have a negative elevation.

Count in 6s, 7s, 9s, 25s and 1,000s

Pages 6–7, 10–11

Counting in steps – step counting – involves recognising and continuing number patterns. We can use known multiplication facts and the relationship between them to help us count in steps.

Counting in steps of 6

When we count in steps, we can often see patterns.

What do you notice about counting in steps of 3 and in steps of 6?

3 6 9 12 15 18 21 24 27 30   6 12 18 24 30

Counting from 0 in 3s gives the **multiples of 3** in the 3 multiplication table.

Counting from 0 in 6s gives the **multiples of 6** in the 6 multiplication table.

What do you notice about the numbers on this number line?

| 0 | 6 | 12 | 18 | 24 | 30 | 36 | 42 | 48 | 54 | 60 |

Say
- **Count on** in 6s from 0 to 60.
- **Count back** in 6s from 60 to 0.
- Choose numbers other than 0 and 60 and count on and back in steps of 6.

Counting in steps of 7

What do you notice about the numbers on this number line?

Counting from 0 in 7s gives the **multiples of 7** in the 7 multiplication table.

| 0 | 7 | 14 | 21 | 28 | 35 | 42 | 49 | 56 | 63 | 70 |

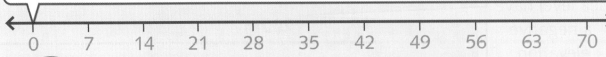

Say
- Count on in 7s from 0 to 70.
- Count back in 7s from 70 to 0.
- Choose numbers other than 0 and 70 and count on and back in steps of 7.

Counting in steps of 9

What do you notice about the numbers on this number line?

Counting from 0 in 9s gives the **multiples of 9** in the 9 multiplication table.

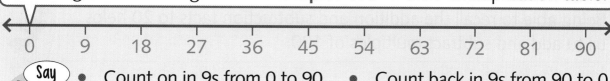

0 9 18 27 36 45 54 63 72 81 90

Say
- Count on in 9s from 0 to 90.
- Count back in 9s from 90 to 0.
- Choose numbers other than 0 and 90 and count on and back in steps of 9.

Counting in steps of 25

Look at these three number lines. How are they the same?

How are they different? What patterns do you notice?

What is the link between the multiples of 25, 50 and 100?

Say

Count on and back in steps of 25, 50 and 100.

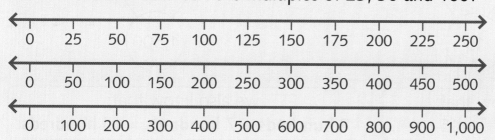

0 25 50 75 100 125 150 175 200 225 250

0 50 100 150 200 250 300 350 400 450 500

0 100 200 300 400 500 600 700 800 900 1,000

Counting in steps of 1,000

Look at this number grid. It shows the 3- and 4-digit multiples of 100.

What patterns do you notice?

100	200	300	400	500	600	700	800	900	1,000
1,100	1,200	1,300	1,400	1,500	1,600	1,700	1,800	1,900	2,000
2,100	2,200	2,300	2,400	2,500	2,600	2,700	2,800	2,900	3,000
3,100	3,200	3,300	3,400	3,500	3,600	3,700	3,800	3,900	4,000
4,100	4,200	4,300	4,400	4,500	4,600	4,700	4,800	4,900	5,000
5,100	5,200	5,300	5,400	5,500	5,600	5,700	5,800	5,900	6,000
6,100	6,200	6,300	6,400	6,500	6,600	6,700	6,800	6,900	7,000
7,100	7,200	7,300	7,400	7,500	7,600	7,700	7,800	7,900	8,000
8,100	8,200	8,300	8,400	8,500	8,600	8,700	8,800	8,900	9,000
9,100	9,200	9,300	9,400	9,500	9,600	9,700	9,800	9,900	10,000

Say
- Choose a number on the grid and count on in steps of 1,000.
- Choose a number on the grid and count back in steps of 1,000.

Use the grid to count on and back in steps of 100.

Pages 26–35

Use known addition and subtraction facts

Pages 6-9, 12-13

Being able to recall the addition and subtraction facts to 20 helps us to add and subtract multiples of 100.

$800 + 700 = \boxed{1,500}$ We can use the known fact 8 + 7 = 15 to help.

Change the **ones** to **hundreds**.

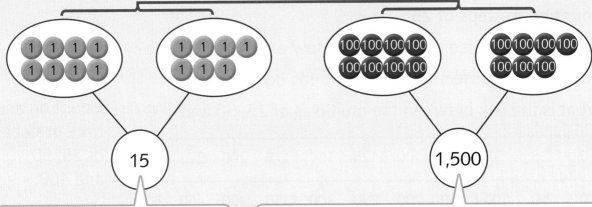

If we know that:	we also know that:
8 **ones** + 7 **ones** = 15 **ones**.	8 **hundreds** + 7 **hundreds** = 15 **hundreds**.
$8 + 7 = 15$	$800 + 700 = 1,500$

- Addition can be done in any order – it's commutative.
- Fact families – addition and subtraction – are related. If we know one addition or subtraction fact, we know three other related facts.

Remember

So,

8 + 7 = 15	800 + 700 = 1,500
7 + 8 = 15	700 + 800 = 1,500
15 − 7 = 8	1,500 − 700 = 800
15 − 8 = 7	1,500 − 800 = 700

and

$1,400 - 600 = \boxed{800}$ ◁ We can use the known fact $14 - 6 = 8$ to help.

Change the **ones** to **hundreds**.

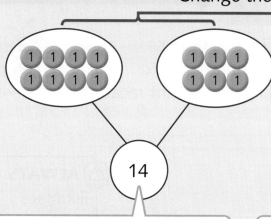
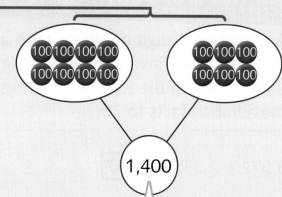

If we know that:
14 **ones** − 6 **ones** = 8 **ones**.

$14 - 6 = 8$

we also know that:
14 **hundreds** − 6 **hundreds** = 8 **hundreds**.

$1,400 - 600 = 800$

Say

If you know that $1,400 - 600 = 800$, what other addition and subtraction facts do you know?

Complete the part-whole models and the missing numbers in the calculations.

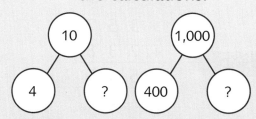

$4 + \boxed{} = 10$

$\boxed{} + 4 = 10$

$10 - \boxed{} = 4$

$10 - 4 = \boxed{}$

$400 + \boxed{} = 1,000$

$\boxed{} + 400 = 1,000$

$1,000 - \boxed{} = 400$

$1,000 - 400 = \boxed{}$

Build

Draw

Use objects or draw a model to show the answers to these calculations.

$500 + 900 = \boxed{}$

$1,700 - 600 = \boxed{}$

Write

If you know each of these answers, what other related facts do you know?

Pages 26-29

Add numbers with up to 4 digits

Pages 6-9, 12-13, 18-19, 22-25

Adding two 4-digit numbers, such as 3,572 + 2,385 or 4,685 + 2,746, involves partitioning 4-digit numbers into thousands, hundreds, tens and ones, and having instant recall of the addition facts to 20.

3,572 + 2,385 = 5,957

⚠ ALWAYS:
Estimate
Calculate
Check

First partition both numbers into thousands, **hundreds**, tens and ones.

Finally combine the ones, tens, **hundreds** and thousands.

1,000s	100s	10s	1s
1,000 1,000 1,000	100 100 100 100 100	10 10 10 10 10 / 10 10	1 1
1,000 1,000	100 100 100	10 10 10 10 10 / 10 10 10	1 1 1 1 1
	100		

Then add the ones.

Next add the tens. As there are more than 10 tens, we need to regroup 10 tens into 1 **hundred**.

Now add the thousands.

Then add the **hundreds**.

We can record this in columns.

```
    3 5 7 2
  + 2 3 8 5
  ─────────
          7
      1 5 0
      8 0 0
    5 0 0 0
  ─────────
    5 9 5 7
```

leads to

```
    3 5 7 2
  + 2 3 8 5
  ─────────
    5 9 5 7
        1
```

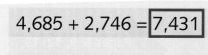

$4,685 + 2,746 = \boxed{7,431}$

First partition both numbers into **thousands**, **hundreds**, tens and ones.

Then add the ones. As there are more than 10 ones, we need to regroup 10 ones into 1 ten.

Finally combine the ones, tens, **hundreds** and **thousands**.

1,000s	100s	10s	1s
1,000 1,000 1,000 1,000	100 100 100 100 100 / 100	10 10 10 10 10 / 10 10 10	1 1 1 1 1
1,000 1,000	100 100 100 100 100 / 100 100	10 10 10 10	1 1 1 1 1 / 1
1,000	100	10	

Now add the **thousands**.

Then add the **hundreds**. As there are more than 10 **hundreds**, we need to regroup 10 **hundreds** into 1 **thousand**.

Next add the tens. As there are more than 10 tens, we need to regroup 10 tens into 1 **hundred**.

We can record this in columns.

```
    4 6 8 5
 +  2 7 4 6
        1 1
      1 2 0
    1 3 0 0
    6 0 0 0
    7 4 3 1
```

leads to

```
    4 6 8 5
 +  2 7 4 6
    7 4 3 1
    1 1 1
```

Use your preferred method to work out the answers to these calculations.

5,347 + 3,800 = ☐

2,345 + 1,748 + 2,059 = ☐

6,249 + 362 = ☐

254 + 1,845 + 84 = ☐

Subtract numbers with up to 4 digits

Pages 6–9, 12–13, 18–19, 22–25

Subtracting two 4-digit numbers, such as 5,628 – 1,275 or 8,637 – 5,879, involves partitioning 4-digit numbers into thousands, hundreds, tens and ones, and having instant recall of the subtraction facts to 20.

5,628 – 1,275 = **4,353**

⚠ **ALWAYS:**
Estimate
Calculate
Check

First partition 5,628 into thousands, hundreds, tens and ones.

Finally place the partitioned number back together.

Then subtract the ones.

1,000s	100s	10s	1s

Now subtract the thousands.

Then subtract the hundreds.

Next subtract the tens. There are 2 tens in 5,628 and we need to subtract 7 tens. As there aren't enough tens in 5,628, exchange 1 hundred for 10 tens.

We can record this in columns.

```
           500    120
  5,000    6̶0̶0̶   2̶0̶    8
– 1,000    200    70     5
  4,000    300    50     3
```

4,000 + 300 + 50 + 3 = 4,353

leads to

```
      5   1
  5 6̶ 2̶ 8
– 1 2 7 5
  4 3 5 3
```

```
      5   12
  5 6̶ 2̶ 8
– 1 2 7 5
  4 3 5 3
```

You can also write the exchanged values like this.

 $8,637 - 5,879 = \boxed{2,758}$

First partition 8,637 into **thousands**, **hundreds**, tens and ones.

Finally place the partitioned number back together.

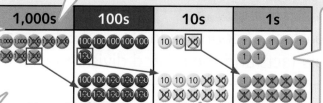

1,000s	100s	10s	1s

Then subtract the ones. There are 7 ones in 8,637 and we need to subtract 9 ones. As there aren't enough ones in 8,637, exchange 1 ten for 10 ones.

Now subtract the thousands.

Then subtract the **hundreds**. There are 6 **hundreds** in 8,637 and we need to subtract 8 **hundreds**. As there aren't enough **hundreds** in 8,637, exchange 1 thousand for 10 **hundreds**.

Next subtract the tens. There are 3 tens in 8,637 and we need to subtract 7 tens. As there aren't enough tens in 8,637, exchange 1 **hundred** for 10 tens.

We can record this in columns.

7,000	1,500	120	17
8,000	600	30	7
− 5,000	800	70	9
2,000	700	50	8

leads to

$$2,000 + 700 + 50 + 8 = 2,758$$

7	15	12	1
8	6	3	7
− 5	8	7	9
2	7	5	8

7	15	12	17
8	6	3	7
− 5	8	7	9
2	7	5	8

You can also write the exchanged values like this.

 Use your preferred method to work out the answers to these calculations.

$8,000 - 4,626 = \boxed{}$

$6,348 - 3,999 = \boxed{}$

$5,381 - 2,100 = \boxed{}$

$7,532 - 641 = \boxed{}$

6 multiplication table

Pages 22–23

We can use the pattern of counting in steps of 6 to recall the 6 multiplication table facts and the related division facts.

How many dots are there **altogether**?

We can **count on in 6s** to find out how many dots there are.

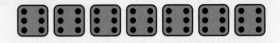

1 **group of** 6 is 6.	3 **groups of** 6 are 18.	5 **groups of** 6 are 30.	7 **groups of** 6 are 42.

There are 7 groups of 6 dots. There are 42 dots altogether.

0 6 12 18 24 30 36 42 48 54 60 66 72

2 groups of 6 are 12.	4 groups of 6 are 24.	6 groups of 6 are 36.

We can also write this as a **multiplication** calculation: $7 \times 6 = 42$

One 6 is 6.

$1 \times 6 = 6$

Two 6s are 12.

$2 \times 6 = 12$

Three 6s are 18.

$3 \times 6 = 18$

Four 6s are 24.

$4 \times 6 = 24$

Five 6s are 30.

$5 \times 6 = 30$

We can say:

7 **lots of** 6 is 42.

7 **times** 6 is 42.

Seven **6s** are 42.

7 **multiplied by** 6 is 42.

The **product** of 7 and 6 is 42.

The products of the 6 multiplication table are called the **multiples of 6**.

We can use the **inverse relationship** between multiplication and division to help us recall the 6 **multiplication facts** and the related **division facts**.

Remember

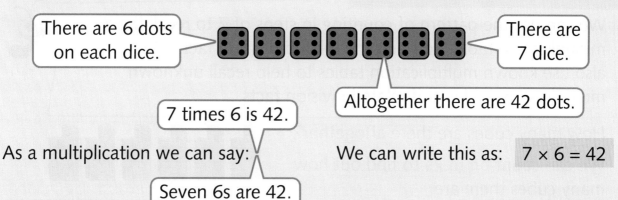

There are 6 dots on each dice.

There are 7 dice.

Altogether there are 42 dots.

7 times 6 is 42.

As a multiplication we can say:

Seven 6s are 42.

We can write this as: $7 \times 6 = 42$

As a division we can say:

42 **divided** by 6 is 7.

We can write this as: $42 \div 6 = 7$

We can use a number line to recall the 6 multiplication table facts and related division facts.

2 times 6 is 12.

5 times 6 is 30.

9 times 6 is 54.

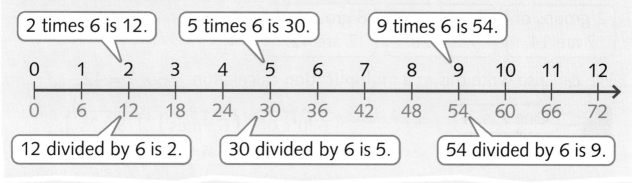

12 divided by 6 is 2.

30 divided by 6 is 5.

54 divided by 6 is 9.

What patterns do you notice?

What do you notice about the multiples of 6 and the multiples of 3?

What is the link between the 3 and 6 multiplication tables?

What is the link between multiplying by 6 and **doubling**?

1	2	3	4	5	6	7	8	9	10
11	12	13	14	15	16	17	18	19	20
21	22	23	24	25	26	27	28	29	30
31	32	33	34	35	36	37	38	39	40
41	42	43	44	45	46	47	48	49	50
51	52	53	54	55	56	57	58	59	60
61	62	63	64	65	66	67	68	69	70
71	72	73	74	75	76	77	78	79	80
81	82	83	84	85	86	87	88	89	90
91	92	93	94	95	96	97	98	99	100

Pages 32-55, 58-61

7 multiplication table

Pages 22-23, 30-31

We can use the pattern of counting in steps of 7 to recall the 7 multiplication table facts and the related division facts. We can also use known multiplication tables to help recall unknown multiplication tables and related division facts.

How many cubes are there **altogether**?

We can **count on in 7s** to find out how many cubes there are.

1 **group of** 7 is 7.	3 groups of 7 are 21.	5 groups of 7 are 35.

There are 6 groups of 7 cubes. There are 42 cubes altogether.

0 7 14 21 28 35 42 49 56 63 70 77 84

2 groups of 7 are 14.	4 groups of 7 are 28.	6 groups of 7 are 42.

We can also write this as a **multiplication** calculation: $6 \times 7 = 42$

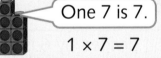

One 7 is 7.

$1 \times 7 = 7$

6 **lots of** 7 is 42.	6 **times** 7 is 42.	Six **7s** are 42.

Two 7s are 14.

$2 \times 7 = 14$

6 **multiplied by** 7 is 42.

We can say:

Three 7s are 21.

$3 \times 7 = 21$

The **product** of 6 and 7 is 42.

Four 7s are 28.

$4 \times 7 = 28$

The products of the 7 multiplication table are called the **multiples of 7**.

Five 7s are 35.

$5 \times 7 = 35$

We can use the **inverse relationship** between multiplication and division to help us recall the 7 **multiplication table facts** and the related **division facts**.

Remember

There are 7 cubes in each block.

There are 6 blocks.

Altogether there are 42 cubes.

6 times 7 is 42.

As a multiplication we can say:

We can write this as: 6 × 7 = 42

Six 7s are 42.

As a division we can say:

42 **divided by** 7 is 6.

We can write this as: 42 ÷ 7 = 6

We can use a number line to recall the 7 multiplication table facts and related division facts.

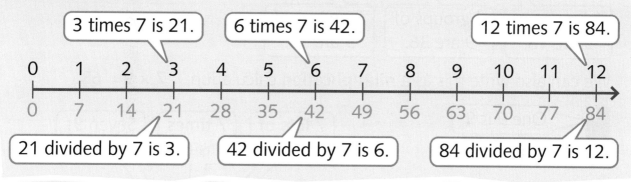

3 times 7 is 21.

6 times 7 is 42.

12 times 7 is 84.

| 0 | 1 | 2 | 3 | 4 | 5 | 6 | 7 | 8 | 9 | 10 | 11 | 12 |
| 0 | 7 | 14 | 21 | 28 | 35 | 42 | 49 | 56 | 63 | 70 | 77 | 84 |

21 divided by 7 is 3.

42 divided by 7 is 6.

84 divided by 7 is 12.

Look at the number line on page 30 showing 7 groups of 6 and the calculation: 7 × 6 = 42

How is the number line and calculation on page 30 the same as the number line and calculation on page 32 showing 6 groups of 7 and 6 × 7 = 42 ?

How is it different?

- Multiplication is **commutative** – it can be done in any order.

Remember

- Multiplication and division are related. If we know one multiplication or division fact then we know three other related facts.

Pages 34–55, 58–61

33

9 multiplication table

Pages 22-23, 30-33

We can use the pattern of counting in steps of 9 and known multiplication tables to recall the 9 multiplication table facts and the related division facts.

How many cubes are there **altogether**?

We can **count on in 9s** to find out how many cubes there are.

> There are 7 groups of 9 cubes. There are 63 cubes altogether.

| 1 **group** of 9 is 9. | 3 groups of 9 are 27. | 5 groups of 9 are 45. | 7 groups of 9 are 63. |

0   9   18   27   36   45   54   63   72   81   90   99   108

| 2 groups of 9 are 18. | 4 groups of 9 are 36. | 6 groups of 9 are 54. |

We can also write this as a **multiplication** calculation: $7 \times 9 = 63$

One 9 is 9.
$1 \times 9 = 9$

Two 9s are 18.
$2 \times 9 = 18$

Three 9s are 27.
$3 \times 9 = 27$

Four 9s are 36.
$4 \times 9 = 36$

Five 9s are 45.
$5 \times 9 = 45$

We can say:

| 7 **lots of** 9 is 63. | 7 **times** 9 is 63. | Seven **9s** are 63. |

7 **multiplied** by 9 is 63.

The **product** of 7 and 9 is 63.

The products of the 9 multiplication table are called the **multiples of 9**.

There are 9 cubes in each block.

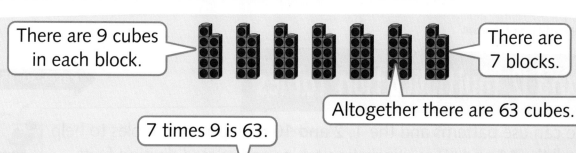

There are 7 blocks.

Altogether there are 63 cubes.

7 times 9 is 63.

As a multiplication we can say:

Seven 9s are 63.

We can write this as: $7 \times 9 = 63$

As a **division** we can say:

63 **divided by** 9 is 7.

We can write this as: $63 \div 9 = 7$

We can use a number line to recall the 9 multiplication table facts and related division facts.

2 times 9 is 18.

7 times 9 is 63.

10 times 9 is 90.

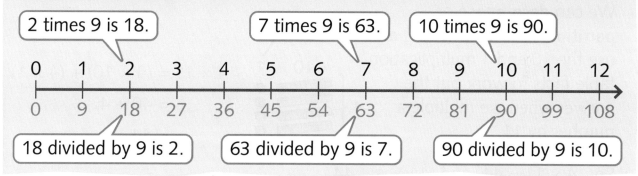

18 divided by 9 is 2.

63 divided by 9 is 7.

90 divided by 9 is 10.

We can use knowledge of the 2, 3, 4, 5, 6, 7, 8 and 10 multiplication tables to help become fluent in the 9 multiplication table.

If we know that $6 \times 9 = 54$ and $9 \times 6 = 54$ then we also know that

$54 \div 9 = 6$ and $54 \div 6 = 9$.

Look at the multiples of 9 on the number line above. What patterns do you notice?

What links are there between the 3, 6 and 9 multiplication tables?

- Multiplication is **commutative** – it can be done in any order.

Remember

- Multiplication and division are related. If we know one multiplication or division fact then we know three other related facts.

Pages 36–55, 58–61

11 and 12 multiplication tables

Pages 30-35

We can use patterns and the 1, 2 and 10 multiplication tables to help recall the 11 and 12 multiplication tables and related division facts.

- Multiplication is **commutative** – it can be done in any order.
- Multiplication and division are related. If we know one multiplication or division fact then we know three other related facts.

Remember

11 multiplication table

$$4 \times 11 = 44$$

We can **decompose** or **partition** 11 into 10 and 1, and use the 10 and 1 multiplication table facts to work out the answer when we multiple a number by 11.

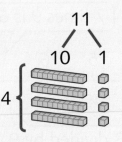

$$4 \times 11 = (4 \times 10) + (4 \times 1)$$
$$= 40 + 4$$
$$= 44$$

So, $4 \times 11 = 44$ and $11 \times 4 = 44$

We also know that $44 \div 11 = 4$ and $44 \div 4 = 11$

We can use a number line to recall the 11 multiplication table facts and related division facts.

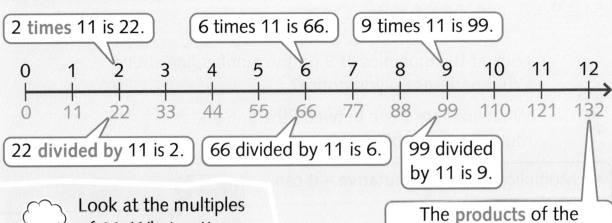

2 times 11 is 22.   6 times 11 is 66.   9 times 11 is 99.

| 0 | 1 | 2 | 3 | 4 | 5 | 6 | 7 | 8 | 9 | 10 | 11 | 12 |

| 0 | 11 | 22 | 33 | 44 | 55 | 66 | 77 | 88 | 99 | 110 | 121 | 132 |

22 divided by 11 is 2.   66 divided by 11 is 6.   99 divided by 11 is 9.

Look at the multiples of 11. What patterns do you notice?

The **products** of the 11 multiplication table are called the **multiples of 11.**

12 multiplication table

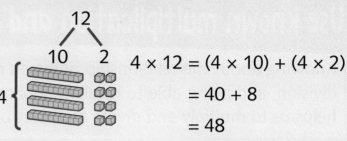

$4 \times 12 = 48$

Like the 11 multiplication table, we can decompose or partition 12 into 10 and 2, and use the 10 and 2 multiplication table facts to work out the answer when we multiple a number by 12.

$4 \times 12 = (4 \times 10) + (4 \times 2)$
$= 40 + 8$
$= 48$

So, $4 \times 12 = 48$ and $12 \times 4 = 48$

We also know that $48 \div 12 = 4$ and $48 \div 4 = 12$

We can use a number line to recall the 12 multiplication table facts and related division facts.

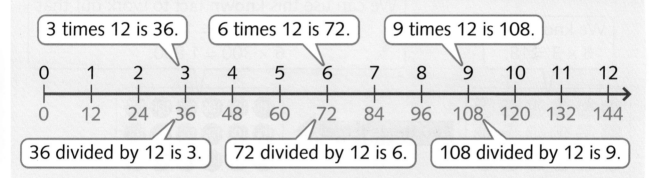

3 times 12 is 36.   6 times 12 is 72.   9 times 12 is 108.

36 divided by 12 is 3.   72 divided by 12 is 6.   108 divided by 12 is 9.

Look at these three number lines.

How are they the same? How are they different?

What patterns do you notice?

What is the link between the 3, 6 and 12 multiplication tables?

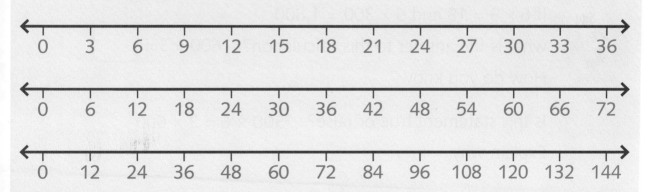

Pages 38-55, 58-61

Use known multiplication and division facts

Pages 30-37

Knowing about the relationship between multiplication and division, and being able to recall multiplication and division facts, helps us to multiply and divide multiples of 100.

- Multiplication is commutative – it can be done in any order.
- Multiplication and division are related. If we know one multiplication or division fact then we know three other related facts.

Remember

We know that
6 × 3 = 18.

We can use this known fact to work out that
6 × 3 hundreds = 18 hundreds
6 × 300 = 1,800.

100 times larger

As one of the numbers in the calculation is 100 times larger, then …

6 × 3 = 18

6 × 300 = 1,800

… the answer is also 100 times larger.

 Say

If 6 × 3 = 18 and 6 × 300 = 1,800

what is the answer to this calculation?   600 × 3 = ☐

How do you know?

Is this statement true or false?   300 × 6 = 3 × 600

Explain why.

There are 18 **hundreds**.
18 **hundreds** divided into **groups of** 3 **hundreds** = 6
1,800 ÷ 300 = 6

We can also see:
18 **hundreds** **divided into** 3 **equal parts** = 6 **hundreds**
1,800 ÷ 3 = 600

So,   and   and

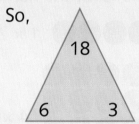   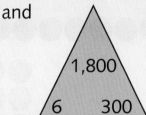   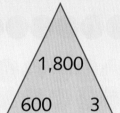

6 × 3 = 18	6 × 300 = 1,800	600 × 3 = 1,800
3 × 6 = 18	300 × 6 = 1,800	3 × 600 = 1,800
18 ÷ 3 = 6	1,800 ÷ 300 = 6	1,800 ÷ 3 = 600
18 ÷ 6 = 3	1,800 ÷ 6 = 300	1,800 ÷ 600 = 3

 What multiplication facts does this
array show?

What are the related division facts?

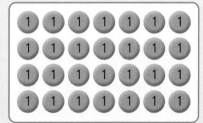

 What multiplication facts does this
array show?

What are the related division facts?

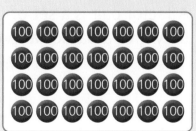

What patterns do you notice about all your
multiplication and division facts?

Pages 40–55

Factor pairs

Pages 30–39

A factor pair is two whole numbers that, when multiplied together, make a particular product. We can use factor pairs to help with multiplication calculations.

Factors are the **whole numbers** that you **multiply** together to get another whole number.

Every whole number has a **factor pair** – even if it's only itself multiplied by 1.

Let's look at these **arrays** and multiplication calculations for the number 20.

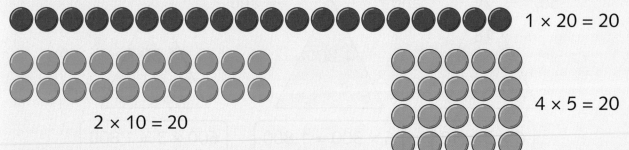

$1 \times 20 = 20$

$2 \times 10 = 20$

$4 \times 5 = 20$

We can see from the arrays that 20 has three factor pairs. It has six factors altogether.

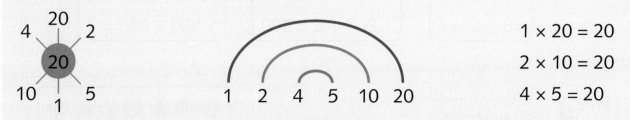

$1 \times 20 = 20$

$2 \times 10 = 20$

$4 \times 5 = 20$

So, the factors of 20 are 1, 2, 4, 5, 10 and 20.

- A **multiple** is the result (or **product**) that we get when one number is multiplied by another number.
- A **factor pair** is a set of two factors. When multiplied together, they give a particular product.

$$\text{factor} \times \text{factor} = \text{product}$$

5 is a factor of 20.

4 is a factor of 20. $4 \times 5 = 20$ 20 is a multiple of 4 and 5.

This multiplication table shows that 18 is in the 2, 3, 6 and 9 multiplication tables.

So, 2, 3, 6 and 9 are all factors of 18.

1 and 18 are also factors of 18.

×	1	2	3	4	5	6	7	8	9	10	11	12
1	1	2	3	4	5	6	7	8	9	10	11	12
2	2	4	6	8	10	12	14	16	⑱	20	22	24
3	3	6	9	12	15	⑱	21	24	27	30	33	36
4	4	8	12	16	20	24	28	32	36	40	44	48
5	5	10	15	20	25	30	35	40	45	50	55	60
6	6	12	⑱	24	30	36	42	48	54	60	66	72
7	7	14	21	28	35	42	49	56	63	70	77	84
8	8	16	24	32	40	48	56	64	72	80	88	96
9	9	⑱	27	36	45	54	63	72	81	90	99	108
10	10	20	30	40	50	60	70	80	90	100	110	120
11	11	22	33	44	55	66	77	88	99	110	121	132
12	12	24	36	48	60	72	84	96	108	120	132	144

We can also think of a factor as a whole number that **divides exactly into** another number.

We can use multiplication and division facts to show this.

1 × 18 = 18 and 18 ÷ 18 = 1

2 × 9 = 18 and 18 ÷ 9 = 2

3 × 6 = 18 and 18 ÷ 6 = 3

So, 1, 2, 3, 6, 9 and 18 are all factors of 18.

Every whole number has at least one factor pair – the number 1 and itself.

Build

Draw

Use objects or draw arrays to show all the factor pairs for each of these numbers.

35   36   48   60

Pages 42-55

Multiply a number by 0, 1, 10 or 100

Pages 6-7, 30-41

Knowing how to multiply a number by 0, 1, 10 and 100 is useful when multiplying larger numbers. It's important to understand what happens to the place value of the digits when you multiply by 10 or 100.

Multiplying by 1 or 0

Look at these 6 tanks. There is 1 fish in each tank.

We can write this as: $6 \times 1 = 6$

The result (or **product**) of **multiplying** a number by 1 is always the number itself.

Look at these 6 tanks with no (or **zero**) fish in each tank.

We can write this as: $6 \times 0 = 0$

The result (or product) of multiplying a number by 0 is always 0.

Multiplying by 10 or 100

When you move up one row on a Gattegno chart, the number becomes **10 times greater**.

When you move up two rows on a Gattegno chart, the number becomes **100 times greater**.

1,000	2,000	3,000	4,000	5,000	6,000	7,000	8,000	9,000
100	200	300	400	500	600	700	800	900
10	20	30	40	50	60	70	80	90
1	2	3	4	5	6	7	8	9

$4 \times 10 = 40$

$8 \times 100 = 800$

We can show multiplying by 10 using place value counters and on a place value chart.

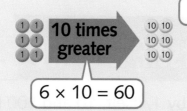

10 times greater

$6 \times 10 = 60$

10 times greater

× 10

1,000s	100s	10s	1s
			7
		7	0

When we **multiply** a **whole number** by 10, the **value** of each **digit** in the number becomes 10 times greater and the digits move one **place value** to the left.

We include a zero in the **ones** place to act as a **place holder**.

Look at these examples of multiplying by 10.

1,000	2,000	3,000	4,000	5,000	6,000	7,000	8,000	9,000
100	200	300	400	500	600	700	800	900
10	20	30	40	50	60	70	80	90
1	2	3	4	5	6	7	8	9

$368 \times 10 = 3,680$

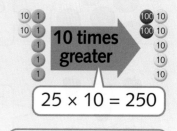

10 times greater

$25 \times 10 = 250$

$279 \times 10 = 2,790$

1,000s	100s	10s	1s
	2	7	9
2	7	9	0

We can show multiplying by 100 using place value counters and on a place value chart.

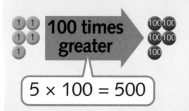

100 times greater

$5 \times 100 = 500$

100 times greater

1,000s	100s	10s	1s
			9
	9	0	0

× 100

When we multiply a whole number by 100, the value of each digit in the number becomes 100 times greater and the digits move two place values to the left.

We include zeros in the **tens** and **ones** places to act as place holders.

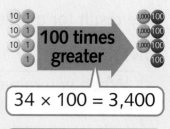

100 times greater

$34 \times 100 = 3,400$

$82 \times 100 = 8,200$

Look at these examples of multiplying by 100.

1,000	2,000	3,000	4,000	5,000	6,000	7,000	8,000	9,000
100	200	300	400	500	600	700	800	900
10	20	30	40	50	60	70	80	90
1	2	3	4	5	6	7	8	9

$47 \times 100 = 4,700$

1,000s	100s	10s	1s
		8	2
8	2	0	0

Pages 44–49, 52–53

Divide a number by 1, itself, 10 or 100

Pages 6-7, 30-43

Knowing how to divide a number by 1, itself, 10 and 100 is useful when dividing larger numbers. It's important to understand what happens to the place value of the digits when you divide by 10 or 100.

Dividing by 1 or itself

6 oranges **shared into** 1 **equal group** is equal to 6.

We can write this as:

$6 \div 1 = 6$

5 apples **divided into** groups of 1 **is equal to** 5.

We can write this as:

$5 \div 1 = 5$

The result (or **quotient**) of **dividing** a number by 1 is always the number itself.

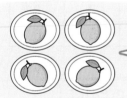

4 lemons shared into 4 equal groups is equal to 1.

We can write this as:

$4 \div 4 = 1$

7 bananas divided into groups of 7 is equal to 1.

We can write this as:

$7 \div 7 = 1$

The result (or quotient) of dividing a number by itself is always 1.

Dividing by 10 or 100

When you move down one row on a Gattegno chart, the number becomes **10 times smaller**.

When you move down two rows on a Gattegno chart, the number becomes **100 times smaller**.

1,000	2,000	3,000	4,000	5,000	6,000	7,000	8,000	9,000
100	200	300	400	500	600	700	800	900
10	20	30	40	50	60	70	80	90
1	2	3	4	5	6	7	8	9

$30 \div 10 = 3$

$700 \div 100 = 7$

We can show dividing by 10 using place value counters and on a place value chart.

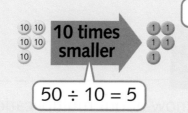

50 ÷ 10 = 5

10 times smaller — ÷ 10

1,000s	100s	10s	1s
		9	0
			9

When we divide a **multiple of 10** by 10, the value of each digit in the number becomes 10 times smaller and the **digits** move one **place value** to the right. We remove the zero from the **ones** place.

Look at these examples of dividing by 10.

1,000	2,000	3,000	4,000	5,000	6,000	7,000	8,000	9,000
100	200	300	400	500	600	700	800	900
10	20	30	40	50	60	70	80	90
1	2	3	4	5	6	7	8	9

2,590 ÷ 10 = 259

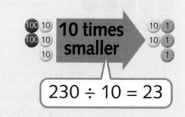

230 ÷ 10 = 23

7,900 ÷ 10 = 790

1,000s	100s	10s	1s
7	9	0	0
	7	9	0

We can show dividing by 100 using place value counters and on a place value chart.

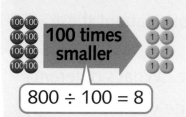

800 ÷ 100 = 8

100 times smaller

1,000s	100s	10s	1s
	4	0	0
			4

÷ 100

When we divide a **multiple of 100** by 100, the value of each digit in the number becomes 100 times smaller and the digits move two place values to the right. We remove the zeros from the **tens** and **ones** places.

Look at these examples of dividing by 100.

1,000	2,000	3,000	4,000	5,000	6,000	7,000	8,000	9,000
100	200	300	400	500	600	700	800	900
10	20	30	40	50	60	70	80	90
1	2	3	4	5	6	7	8	9

3,500 ÷ 100 = 35

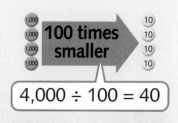

4,000 ÷ 100 = 40

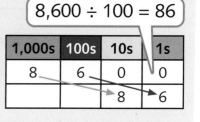

8,600 ÷ 100 = 86

1,000s	100s	10s	1s
8	6	0	0
		8	6

Pages 50–51, 54–55, 70–73

Multiply three numbers

Pages 30-43

We can use and apply what we know about multiplication of two numbers to multiply three numbers together.

This array shows 4 **multiplied by** 5.

We can write this as the **multiplication** calculation: $4 \times 5 = 20$

Now look at these arrays:

These arrays show 2 **groups of** 20.

There are 2 groups of 4 multiplied by 5.

We can write this as the multiplication calculation:

$4 \times 5 \times 2 = 40$

So, 40 is the result (or **product**) of multiplying the three numbers together.

We can work out the product of $4 \times 5 \times 2$ in different ways.

$4 \times 5 \times 2$

$20 \times 2 = 40$

$4 \times 5 \times 2$

$4 \times 10 = 40$

What do you notice about these two methods?

What's the same? What's different?

Which method do you prefer? Why?

Now look at this example.

This array shows 2 multiplied by 3.

There are 4 groups of 2 multiplied by 3.

$2 \times 3 = 6$

$2 \times 3 \times 4 = 24$

$2 \times 3 \times 4$

$6 \times 4 = 24$

$2 \times 3 \times 4$

$2 \times 12 = 24$

Remember **Factors** are the **whole numbers** that we multiply together to get another whole number.

Look at these two pairs of calculations again.

$4 \times 5 \times 2 = 20 \times 2$ $2 \times 3 \times 4 = 6 \times 4$
$\qquad\qquad = 40$ $\qquad\qquad\quad = 24$

$4 \times 5 \times 2 = 4 \times 10$ $2 \times 3 \times 4 = 2 \times 12$
$\qquad\qquad = 40$ $\qquad\qquad\quad = 24$

Changing the grouping of the factors does not change the product.

This is called the **associative property**.

When we multiply three numbers together, we can use **commutativity** to change the order of the factors to multiply them in a way that makes the calculation more efficient.

Multiplication is **commutative** – it can be done in any order. **Remember**

Let's look again at the calculation $4 \times 5 \times 2 = 40$.

What do you notice about the six calculations below?

What's the same? What's different?

Which calculation do you find easiest to answer? Why is this?

$4 \times 5 \times 2 = 40$	$5 \times 4 \times 2 = 40$	$2 \times 5 \times 4 = 40$
$4 \times 2 \times 5 = 40$	$5 \times 2 \times 4 = 40$	$2 \times 4 \times 5 = 40$

Build **Draw**

Use objects or draw arrays to find the product for each of these calculations.

Choose which order to group the numbers to make it easier to calculate effectively.

$6 \times 2 \times 4 = \boxed{}$ $3 \times 8 \times 5 = \boxed{}$ $3 \times 7 \times 2 = \boxed{}$

Pages 48–49, 52–53

Pages 6-9, 18-19, 30-43, 46-47

Multiply a 2-digit number by a 1-digit number

We can use our understanding of place value and multiplication tables facts to multiply a 2-digit number by a 1-digit number, such as 34 × 2 or 73 × 6.

We can represent this multiplication **calculation** using place value counters.

ALWAYS:
Estimate
Calculate
Check

As we are multiplying 34 by 2, first **partition** 2 lots of 34 into tens and ones.

Then **multiply** the ones. 4 ones multiplied by 2 (4 × 2).

Next multiply the tens. 3 tens multiplied by 2 (30 × 2).

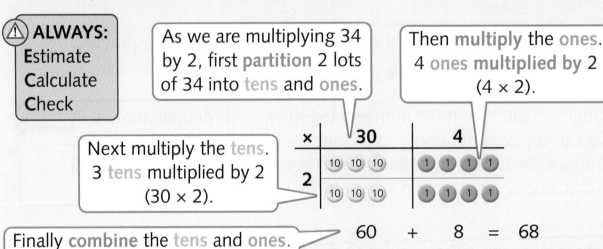

Finally **combine** the tens and ones.

60 + 8 = 68

We can record this calculation in different ways.

Grid method

×	30	4	
2	60	8	= 68

Partitioning method

34 × 2 = (30 × 2) + (4 × 2)
= 60 + 8
= 68

Expanded written method

```
    3 4
  ×   2
      8   (4 × 2)
    6 0   (30 × 2)
    6 8
```

leads to

Formal written method of short multiplication

```
    3 4
  ×   2
    6 8
```

What's the same about each of these methods?

What's different?

Which method do you prefer? Why?

$73 \times 6 = \boxed{438}$

Step 1: Set out the calculation.

> As we are multiplying 73 by 6, first partition 6 lots of 73 into tens and ones.

×	70	3
6	10 10 10 10 10 10 10 10 10 10 10 10 10 10 10 10 10 10 10 10 10 10 10 10 10 10 10 10 10 10 10 10 10 10 10 10 10 10 10 10 10 10	1 1 1 1 1 1 1 1 1 1 1 1 1 1 1 1 1 1

Step 2: Multiply the ones.

> 3 ones multiplied by 6 (3 × 6 = 18). As there are more than 10 ones, we need to regroup 10 ones into 1 ten.

×	70	3
6	10 10 10 10 10 10 10 10 10 10 10 10 10 10 10 10 10 10 10 10 10 10 10 10 10 10 10 10 10 10 10 10 10 10 10 10 10 10 10 10 10 10	1 1 1 1 1 1 1 1 1 1 1 1 1 1 1 1 1 1

10

Step 3: Multiply the tens.

> 7 tens multiplied by 6 (70 × 6 = 420). As there are more than 10 tens, we need to regroup 40 tens into 4 **hundreds**.

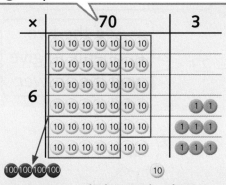

100 100 100 100   10

Step 4: Combine the hundreds, tens and ones.

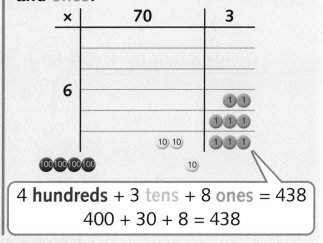

> 4 **hundreds** + 3 tens + 8 ones = 438
> 400 + 30 + 8 = 438

We can record this calculation in different ways.

Grid method

×	70	3	
6	420	18	= 438

Expanded written method

```
  7 3
×   6
  1 8   (3 × 6)
4 2 0   (70 × 6)
4 3 8
```

leads to

Partitioning method

73 × 6 = (70 × 6) + (3 × 6)

= 420 + 18

= 438

Formal written method of short multiplication

```
  7 3        7 3
×   6      × ₁ 6
4 3 8      4 3 8
  1
```

> You can also write the regrouped value like this.

What's the same about each of these methods?

What's different?

Which method do you prefer? Why?

Pages 52–53

Divide a 2-digit number by a 1-digit number

Pages 6–9, 18–19, 30–41, 44–45

We can use our understanding of place value and multiplication and division facts to divide a 2-digit number by a 1-digit number, such as $92 \div 4$.

Each part of a **division** calculation has a special name. It's helpful to know these names.

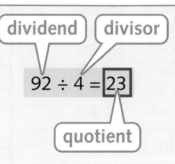

dividend   divisor

$$92 \div 4 = \boxed{23}$$

quotient

⚠ **ALWAYS:**
Estimate
Calculate
Check

We can **decompose** or **regroup** 92.

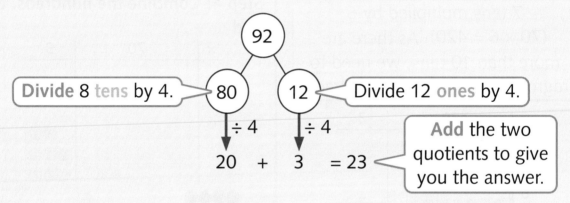

Divide 8 tens by 4. → 80

92

12 ← **Divide 12 ones by 4.**

$\div 4$ $\div 4$

20 + 3 = 23 ← **Add** the two quotients to give you the answer.

Remember We can regroup numbers in different ways.

We can also regroup 92 like this.

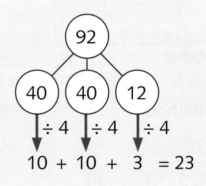

92

40   40   12

$\div 4$ $\div 4$ $\div 4$

10 + 10 + 3 = 23

How else could you regroup 92 to work out the answer to this division calculation?

How does **halving** help when dividing 92 by 2?

How does halving help when dividing 92 by 4?

What about when dividing 92 by 8?

What happens if you divide 92 by 8?

We can represent this with place value counters.

Step 1: Set out the calculation.

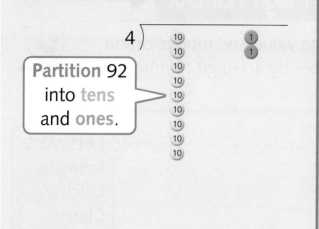

Partition 92 into tens and ones.

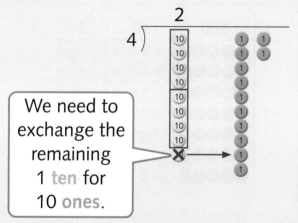

Step 2: Share the tens.

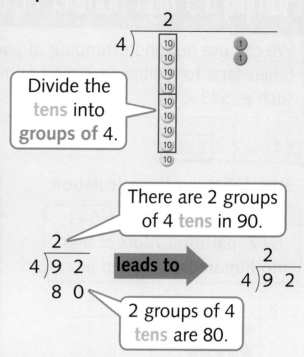

Divide the tens into groups of 4.

There are 2 groups of 4 tens in 90.

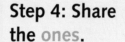

leads to

2 groups of 4 tens are 80.

Step 3: Exchange the tens.

We need to exchange the remaining 1 ten for 10 ones.

$$4 \overline{)92} \quad \text{leads to} \quad 4\overline{)9\,^{1}2}$$

$$\begin{array}{r} 2 \\ 4\overline{)9\ 2} \\ -\ 8\ 0 \\ \hline 1\ 2 \end{array}$$

There are now 12 ones.

Step 4: Share the ones.

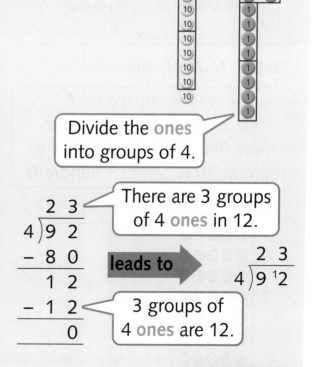

Divide the ones into groups of 4.

There are 3 groups of 4 ones in 12.

$$\begin{array}{r} 2\ 3 \\ 4\overline{)9\ 2} \\ -\ 8\ 0 \\ \hline 1\ 2 \\ -\ 1\ 2 \\ \hline 0 \end{array}$$

leads to

3 groups of 4 ones are 12.

Pages 54–55

51

Multiply a 3-digit number by a 1-digit number

Pages 6-9, 18-19, 30-43, 46-49

We can use our understanding of place value and multiplication tables facts to multiply a 3-digit number by a 1-digit number, such as 543×7.

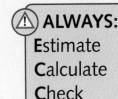

$543 \times 7 = \boxed{3,801}$

⚠ **ALWAYS:**
Estimate
Calculate
Check

Step 1: Set out the calculation.

> As we are multiplying 543 by 7, **partition** 7 lots of 543 into **hundreds**, tens and ones.

×	500	40	3
7	100 100 100 100 100 100 100 100 100 100 100 100 100 100 100 100 100 100 100 100 100 100 100 100 100 100 100 100 100 100 100 100 100 100 100	10 10 10 10 10 10 10 10 10 10 10 10 10 10 10 10 10 10 10 10 10 10 10 10 10 10 10 10	1 1 1 1 1 1 1 1 1 1 1 1 1 1 1 1 1 1 1 1 1

Step 2: Multiply the ones.

> 3 ones multiplied by 7 ($3 \times 7 = 21$). As there are more than 10 ones, we need to **regroup** 20 ones into 2 tens.

×	500	40	3
7	100 100 100 100 100 100 100 100 100 100 100 100 100 100 100 100 100 100 100 100 100 100 100 100 100 100 100 100 100 100 100 100 100 100 100	10 10 10 10 10 10 10 10 10 10 10 10 10 10 10 10 10 10 10 10 10 10 10 10 10 10 10 10	1 1 1 1 1 1 1 1 1 1 1 1 1 1 1 1 1 1 1 1 1
		10 10	

Step 3: Multiply the tens.

> 4 tens multiplied by 7 ($40 \times 7 = 280$). As there are more than 10 tens, we need to regroup 30 tens into 3 **hundreds**.

×	500	40	3
7	100 100 100 100 100 100 100 100 100 100 100 100 100 100 100 100 100 100 100 100 100 100 100 100 100 100 100 100 100 100 100 100 100 100 100	10 10 10 10 10 10 10 10 10 10 10 10 10 10 10 10 10 10 10 10 10 10 10 10 10 10 10 10	 1
	100 100 100	10 10	

Step 4: Multiply the hundreds.

5 **hundreds** multiplied by 7 (500 × 7 = 3,500). As there are more than 10 **hundreds**, we need to regroup 30 **hundreds** into 3 **thousands**.

Step 5: Combine the thousands, hundreds, tens and ones.

3 thousands + 8 **hundreds** + 1 one = 3,801
3,000 + 800 + 1 = 3,801

We can record this calculation in different ways.

Grid method

×	500	40	3	
7	3,500	280	21	= 3,801

Partitioning method

$543 \times 7 = (500 \times 7) + (40 \times 7) + (3 \times 7)$
$= 3,500 + 280 + 21$
$= 3,801$

Expended written method **Expanded written method**

```
    5 4 3
×       7
    2 1   (3 × 7)
  2 8 0   (40 × 7)
3 5 0 0   (500 × 7)
3 8 0 1
  1
```

leads to

Formal written method of short multiplication

```
    5 4 3              5 4 3
×       7         × ₃ ₂ 7
3 8 0 1           3 8 0 1
  ₃ ₂
```

You can also write the regrouped values like this.

What's the same about each of these methods?

What's different?

Which method do you prefer? Why?

Divide a 3-digit number by a 1-digit number

Pages 6-9, 18-19, 30-41, 44-45, 50-51

We can use our understanding of place value and multiplication and division facts to divide a 3-digit number by a 1-digit number, such as 336 ÷ 8.

336 ÷ 8 = 42   We can **decompose** or **regroup** 336.

⚠ **ALWAYS:**
Estimate
Calculate
Check

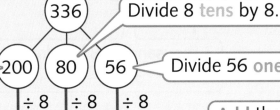

Divide 8 **tens** by 8.

Divide 2 hundreds by 8.

Divide 56 **ones** by 8.

÷ 8   ÷ 8   ÷ 8

25 + 10 + 7 = 42

Add the three **quotients** to give you the answer.

Remember We can regroup numbers in different ways.

We can also regroup 336 like this.

How else could you regroup 336 to work out the answer to this division calculation?

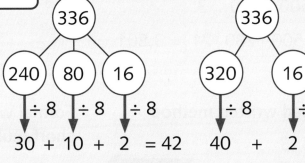

÷ 8   ÷ 8   ÷ 8

30 + 10 + 2 = 42

÷ 8   ÷ 8

40 + 2 = 42

We can represent this with place value counters.

Step 1: Set out the calculation.

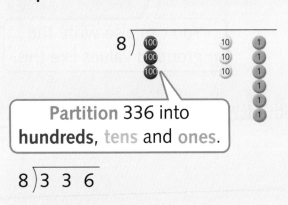

8)

Partition 336 into hundreds, tens and ones.

8) 3 3 6

Step 2: Share the hundreds.

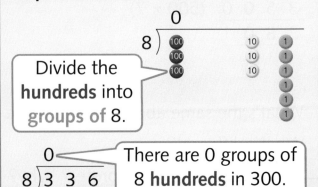

0
8)

Divide the hundreds into groups of 8.

0
8) 3 3 6

There are 0 groups of 8 **hundreds** in 300.

Step 3: Exchange the hundreds.

$$0$$
$$8\overline{)}$$

> We need to exchange the 3 **hundreds** for 30 tens.

$$\begin{array}{r} 0 \\ 8\overline{)3\ \ 3\ \ 6} \end{array}$$ **leads to** $$\begin{array}{r} \\ 8\overline{)3\ {}^{3}3\ \ 6} \end{array}$$

> There are now 33 tens.

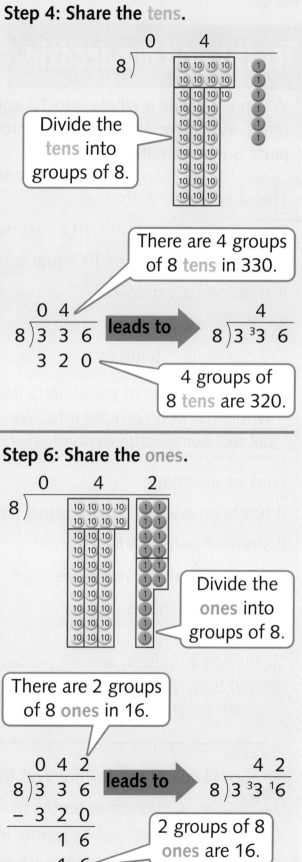

Step 4: Share the tens.

$$\begin{array}{cc} 0 & 4 \end{array}$$
$$8\overline{)}$$

> Divide the tens into groups of 8.

> There are 4 groups of 8 tens in 330.

$$\begin{array}{r} 0\ 4 \\ 8\overline{)3\ \ 3\ \ 6} \\ 3\ 2\ 0 \end{array}$$ **leads to** $$\begin{array}{r} 4 \\ 8\overline{)3\ {}^{3}3\ \ 6} \end{array}$$

> 4 groups of 8 tens are 320.

Step 5: Exchange the tens.

$$\begin{array}{cc} 0 & 4 \end{array}$$
$$8\overline{)}$$

> We need to exchange the remaining 1 ten for 10 ones.

$$\begin{array}{r} 0\ 4 \\ 8\overline{)3\ \ 3\ \ 6} \\ -\ 3\ 2\ 0 \\ \hline 1\ 6 \end{array}$$ **leads to** $$\begin{array}{r} 4 \\ 8\overline{)3\ {}^{3}3\ {}^{1}6} \end{array}$$

> There are now 16 ones.

Step 6: Share the ones.

$$\begin{array}{ccc} 0 & 4 & 2 \end{array}$$
$$8\overline{)}$$

> Divide the ones into groups of 8.

> There are 2 groups of 8 ones in 16.

$$\begin{array}{r} 0\ 4\ 2 \\ 8\overline{)3\ \ 3\ \ 6} \\ -\ 3\ 2\ 0 \\ \hline 1\ 6 \\ -\ 1\ 6 \\ \hline 0 \end{array}$$ **leads to** $$\begin{array}{r} 4\ 2 \\ 8\overline{)3\ {}^{3}3\ {}^{1}6} \end{array}$$

> 2 groups of 8 ones are 16.

Tenths and hundredths

When we divide a whole into 10 equal parts, each of the parts is a tenth. When we divide a whole into 100 equal parts, each of the parts is a hundredth.

This shape represents 1 whole.

It has been divided into 10 equal parts.

Each square is 1 out of 10 equal squares.

It shows 1 part shaded.

So, the shaded part is 1 tenth.

We can write 1 tenth as a fraction.

> The number of parts we are thinking about. We call this number the numerator.

> The total number of equal parts the whole has been divided into. We call this number the denominator.

$$\frac{1}{10}$$

> We call this line the division bar or the vinculum.

Look at this shape.

It has been divided into 10 equal parts.

It shows 7 parts shaded.

So, 7 tenths of this shape are shaded.

We can write this as $\frac{7}{10}$.

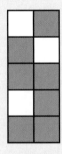

Like whole numbers, we can position tenths on a number line and count on and back in tenths.

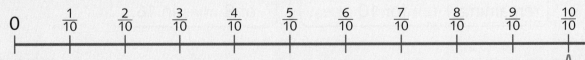

$$0 \quad \frac{1}{10} \quad \frac{2}{10} \quad \frac{3}{10} \quad \frac{4}{10} \quad \frac{5}{10} \quad \frac{6}{10} \quad \frac{7}{10} \quad \frac{8}{10} \quad \frac{9}{10} \quad \frac{10}{10}$$

> $\frac{10}{10}$ equals 1.

Say Look at the fractions on this number line.

- Count on in tenths from 0 to 1.
- Count back in tenths from 1 to 0.
- Starting from a tenth such as $\frac{2}{10}$, count on in tenths to 1.
- Starting from a tenth such as $\frac{8}{10}$, count back in tenths to 0.

This 100 square represents 1 whole.

It has been divided into 100 equal parts.

Each square is 1 out of 100 equal squares.

We can write 1 hundredth as a fraction: $\frac{1}{100}$

Each row (or column) is 1 out of 10 equal rows (or columns).

Look at each of these 100 squares.

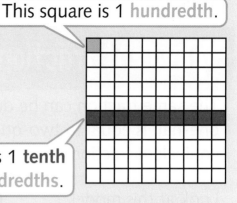

This square is 1 hundredth.

This row is 1 **tenth** or 10 hundredths.

21 parts are shaded. So, 21 hundredths of this shape are shaded. We can write this as $\frac{21}{100}$.

45 parts are shaded. So, 45 hundredths of this shape are shaded. We can write this as $\frac{45}{100}$.

67 parts are shaded. So, 67 hundredths of this shape are shaded. We can write this as $\frac{67}{100}$.

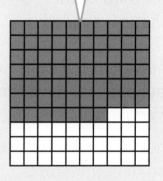

We can **partition** or **regroup** hundredths into **tenths** and **hundredths**.

How else could you regroup each of these fractions into **tenths** and **hundredths**?

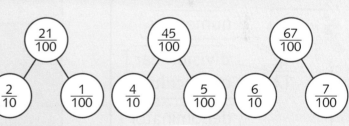

Like whole numbers and **tenths**, we can position hundredths on a number line and count on and back in hundredths.

Use these number lines to count on and back in hundredths.

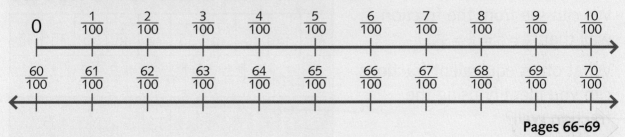

Pages 66-69

Equivalent fractions

Pages 30-37

The same fraction can be described in different ways. For example, one-half is equal to two-quarters. These related fractions are called equivalent fractions.

Look at this model.
There are 12 equal parts.
4 parts are shaded.

We can say that:

We can write this as: $\frac{4}{12}$.

4 twelfths of the shape are shaded.

Look at these models. We can see that: $\frac{1}{3} = \frac{2}{6} = \frac{4}{12}$.

1 third of the shape is shaded.

2 sixths of the shape are shaded.

Equivalent fractions are fractions that have the same, or equal, value.

They have different numerators and denominators.

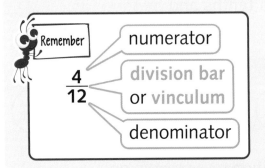

Remember

numerator

division bar or vinculum

$\frac{4}{12}$

denominator

We can use a fraction wall to identify equivalent fractions.

We can see from the fraction wall that: $\frac{1}{3} = \frac{2}{6} = \frac{3}{9} = \frac{4}{12}$.

What other equivalent fractions can you identify using the fraction wall?

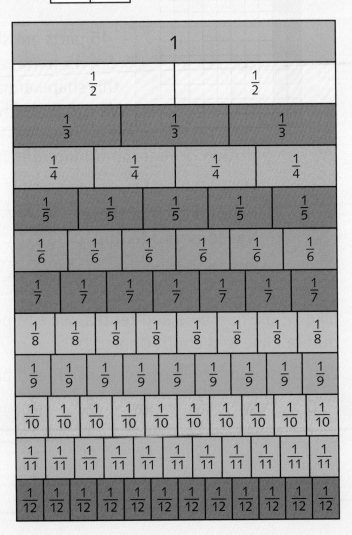

A multiplication grid can make finding equivalent fractions quicker and easier.

Look at the two rows highlighted on this multiplication grid.

> Imagine the line drawn between the two rows is a vinculum, making the two rows into fractions.

> If we read along the two rows, we can see that:
> $\frac{1}{3} = \frac{2}{6} = \frac{3}{9} = \frac{4}{12} \cdots$

> These two rows show all the fractions up to $\frac{12}{36}$ that are equivalent to $\frac{1}{3}$.

×	1	2	3	4	5	6	7	8	9	10	11	12
1	1	2	3	4	5	6	7	8	9	10	11	12
2	2	4	6	8	10	12	14	16	18	20	22	24
3	3	6	9	12	15	18	21	24	27	30	33	36
4	4	8	12	16	20	24	28	32	36	40	44	48
5	5	10	15	20	25	30	35	40	45	50	55	60
6	6	12	18	24	30	36	42	48	54	60	66	72
7	7	14	21	28	35	42	49	56	63	70	77	84
8	8	16	24	32	40	48	56	64	72	80	88	96
9	9	18	27	36	45	54	63	72	81	90	99	108
10	10	20	30	40	50	60	70	80	90	100	110	120
11	11	22	33	44	55	66	77	88	99	110	121	132
12	12	24	36	48	60	72	84	96	108	120	132	144

Use the multiplication table to find fractions that are equivalent to:

$\frac{1}{4}$ $\frac{1}{5}$ $\frac{1}{10}$ $\frac{1}{12}$

What patterns do you notice?

What relationships can you see between the fractions?

What relationships can you see between the numerator and denominator?

Rosie says:

> If I multiply the numerator and denominator of $\frac{1}{5}$ by 2, I will get the equivalent fraction of $\frac{2}{10}$. If I multiply them both by 3, I will get $\frac{3}{15}$.

Is Rosie right? Prove it.

Amari says:

> It is the same for non-unit fractions. If I multiply the numerator and denominator of $\frac{2}{5}$ by 2, I get $\frac{4}{10}$.

Is Amari right? Prove it.

Calculate a fraction of an amount

Pages 30-37

We can find a fraction of an amount by dividing the whole by the denominator and multiplying the quotient by the numerator.

$\frac{1}{3}$ of 18 = 6

To calculate **unit** fractions of an amount:

1. Find the total amount – the **whole**.

2. Divide the whole by the denominator.

Remember

$\frac{1}{3}$ — numerator
— division bar or vinculum
— denominator

We can show this in a model.

18 is the whole.

The whole has been divided into 3 equal groups.

18

1 group is 1 third of the whole.

We can say: 18 divided into 3 equal groups is equal to 6.

We can also say: 1 third of 18 is 6.

When we calculate a fraction of an amount, the denominator of the fraction tells us how many equal groups the whole is divided into.

Divide the whole by the denominator. $\frac{1}{3}$

The numerator of the fraction tells us how many groups of the whole we are finding.

Find the amount in 1 of the groups.

So, to find $\frac{1}{3}$ of 18, we divide 18 by 3. $18 \div 3 = 6$

 Draw Draw models to find:

$\frac{1}{3}$ of 27 = ☐ $\frac{1}{7}$ of 56 = ☐ $\frac{1}{8}$ of 32 = ☐

$\frac{2}{3}$ of 18 = $\boxed{12}$

To calculate **non-unit** fractions of an amount:

1. Find the total amount – the whole.

2. Divide the whole by the denominator.

3. **Multiply** the quotient by the numerator.

We can show this in a model.

18 is the whole.

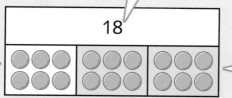

The whole has been divided into 3 equal groups.

18

2 groups are 2 thirds of the whole.

We can say: 18 divided into 3 equal groups is equal to 6. 2 groups of 6 is equal to 12.

We can also say: 2 thirds of 18 equals 12.

So, to find $\frac{2}{3}$ of 18:

- First, divide 18 by 3 to find $\frac{1}{3}$.

Divide the whole by the denominator.

$18 \div 3 = 6$

$\frac{2}{3}$

- Then multiply the quotient by 2 to find the answer.

$6 \times 2 = 12$

Multiply the quotient by the numerator.

 Draw

Draw a model to find: $\frac{1}{10}$ of 40 = ☐

Then use the model to calculate:

$\frac{2}{10}$ of 40 = ☐ $\frac{5}{10}$ of 40 = ☐ $\frac{9}{10}$ of 40 = ☐

$\frac{3}{10}$ of 40 = ☐ $\frac{8}{10}$ of 40 = ☐ $\frac{10}{10}$ of 40 = ☐

What patterns do you notice?

Fractions greater than 1

Fractions are not always less than one whole. We can use fractions to represent the number of parts greater than a whole.

Each of these circles is **divided into** 6 **equal parts** – sixths.

Remember

numerator

$\dfrac{4}{12}$

vinculum

denominator

6 sixths are shaded.

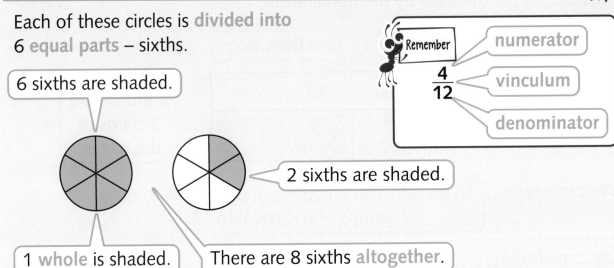

2 sixths are shaded.

1 **whole** is shaded.

There are 8 sixths **altogether**.

So, 8 sixths = 1 whole + 2 sixths.

We can represent this in a part-whole model.

There are 8 sixths altogether.

$\dfrac{8}{6}$

8 sixths = 1 whole + 2 sixths.

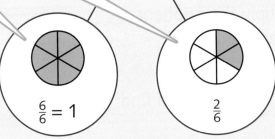

$\dfrac{6}{6} = 1$

$\dfrac{2}{6}$

Look at these models. They have each been divided into 5 equal parts – fifths.

5 fifths

5 fifths

2 fifths

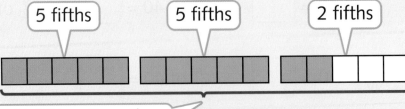

There are 12 fifths altogether.

As we know that 5 fifths **equal** 1 whole, then:
12 fifths = 2 wholes + 2 fifths.

We can write how many fifths there are altogether in two different ways:

$\dfrac{12}{5}$

> This is called an **improper fraction**. In an improper fraction, the numerator is **greater than**, or **equal to**, the denominator.

is the same as:

$2\dfrac{2}{5}$

> This is called a **mixed number**. A mixed number is a number that is made up of a **whole number** and a **fraction**.

$\dfrac{12}{5}$ We say: 12 fifths

$2\dfrac{2}{5}$ We say: 2 and 2 fifths

Say Use these number lines to count on and back in mixed numbers.

Continue the count beyond 3.

Write Write each of these as an improper fraction and as a mixed number.

Pages 64-65

Add and subtract fractions greater than 1

Pages 62–63

We can apply our understanding of addition and subtraction of proper fractions (fractions less than 1) to adding and subtracting fractions greater than 1.

When we **add** fractions with the **same denominator**, the denominators stay the same. We just add the **numerators**, and any **whole numbers**, to find out how many **parts** there are **altogether**.

Add two improper fractions

$$\frac{6}{4} + \frac{5}{4} = \boxed{\frac{11}{4}} = \boxed{2\frac{3}{4}}$$

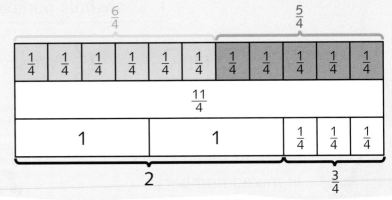

Add a proper fraction to a mixed number

$$1\frac{2}{5} + \frac{4}{5} = \boxed{1\frac{6}{5}} = \boxed{2\frac{1}{5}}$$

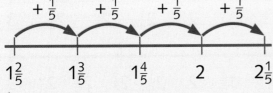

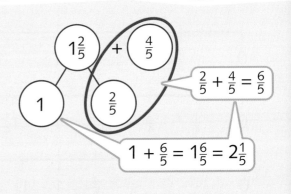

Add two mixed numbers

$$3\frac{6}{7} + 2\frac{3}{7} = \boxed{5\frac{9}{7}} = \boxed{6\frac{2}{7}}$$

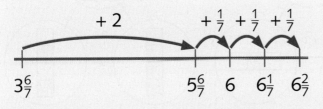

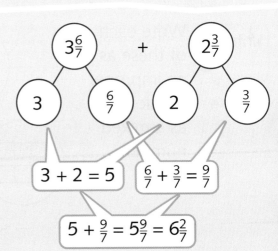

When we **subtract** fractions with the same denominator, the denominators stay the same. We just subtract the numerators to find out how many parts of the whole are **left**.

Subtract two improper fractions

$\frac{9}{5} - \frac{7}{5} = \boxed{\frac{2}{5}}$

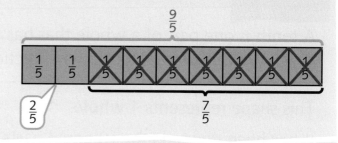

Subtract a proper fraction from a whole number

$3 - \frac{4}{5} = \boxed{2\frac{1}{5}}$

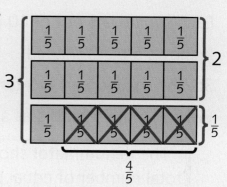

Subtract a proper fraction from a mixed number

$2\frac{2}{7} - \frac{5}{7} = \boxed{1\frac{4}{7}}$

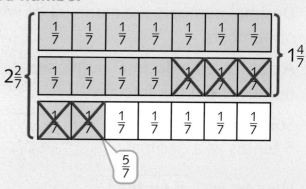

Subtract two mixed numbers

$4\frac{5}{8} - 2\frac{2}{8} = \boxed{2\frac{3}{8}}$

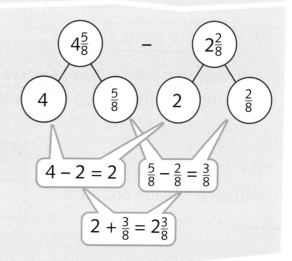

$4 - 2 = 2$ $\qquad$ $\frac{5}{8} - \frac{2}{8} = \frac{3}{8}$

$2 + \frac{3}{8} = 2\frac{3}{8}$

Tenths

Pages 56–57

A tenth is one part of a whole that has been divided into 10 equal parts. We can express tenths as a fraction or as a decimal.

This shape represents 1 **whole**.

It has been **divided into** 10 **equal parts**.

Each square is 1 out of 10 equal squares.

It shows 5 parts shaded.

So, the shaded part is 5 **tenths**.

We can write 5 **tenths** as a **fraction**.

> The **denominator** shows the total number of equal parts the whole has been divided into.

$$\frac{5}{10}$$

> The **numerator** shows the number of parts we are thinking about.

Decimal numbers are made up of **whole numbers** and fractions of numbers.

A dot, called a **decimal point**, separates the whole number from the fraction.

So, we can also write 5 **tenths** as a decimal.

> whole number

0.5

> part of the whole (fractional part) – tenths

> decimal point

We say: > 5 tenths

or > zero point five

Just like with whole numbers, we can represent **tenths** using a place value grid.

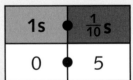

We can also represent this with place value counters.

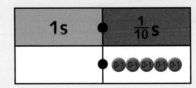

Look at these decimals represented using place value grids and part-whole models.

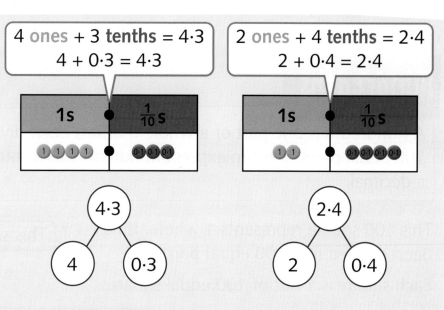

4 ones + 3 tenths = 4·3
4 + 0·3 = 4·3

2 ones + 4 tenths = 2·4
2 + 0·4 = 2·4

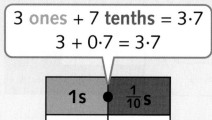

3 ones + 7 tenths = 3·7
3 + 0·7 = 3·7

1 ten + 5 ones + 6 tenths = 15·6
10 + 5 + 0·6 = 15·6

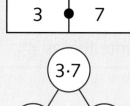

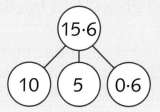

How else could you **partition** (or **regroup**) each of these decimals?

Like with whole numbers, we can position **tenths** on a number line and count on and back in **tenths**.

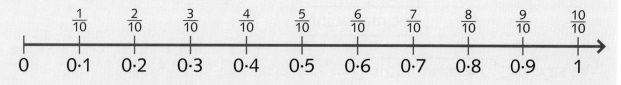

 Draw Draw a place value grid, place value counters or a part-whole model to represent each of these decimals.

0·9   2·8

1·5   14·2

 Write For each decimal, what is the value of each of its digits?

Pages 68–71, 74–77

Hundredths

Pages 56-57, 66-67

A hundredth is one part of a whole that has been divided into 100 equal parts. We can express hundredths as a fraction or as a decimal.

This 100 square represents 1 **whole**. It has been **divided into** 100 **equal parts**.

Each square is 1 out of 100 equal squares.

We can write 1 hundredth as a **fraction**: $\dfrac{1}{100}$

Each row (or column) is 1 out of 10 equal rows (or columns).

This square is 1 hundredth.

This row is 1 **tenth** or 10 hundredths.

So, $\dfrac{1}{10} = \dfrac{10}{100}$

There are 24 green squares in this 100 square. 24 hundredths are shaded green. As a fraction, we write this as $\dfrac{24}{100}$.

We can also write 24 hundredths as a **decimal**.

part of the whole (fractional part) – **tenths**

whole number → 0·24 ← part of the whole (fractional part) – hundredths

decimal point

We say: 24 hundredths

or zero point two four

We can represent hundredths using a place value grid and place value counters.

1s		$\frac{1}{10}$ s	$\frac{1}{100}$ s
		0·1 0·1	0·01 0·01 0·01 0·01

Look at these decimals represented using place value grids and part-whole models.

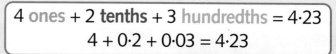

4 **ones** + 2 **tenths** + 3 **hundredths** = 4·23
4 + 0·2 + 0·03 = 4·23

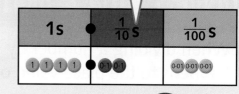

2 **ones** + 3 **tenths** + 1 **hundredth** = 2·31
2 + 0·3 + 0·01 = 2·31

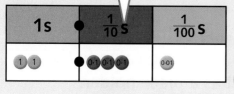

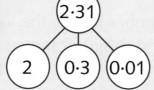

2·31 = 2, 0·3, 0·01

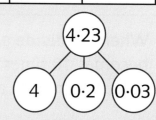

4·23 = 4, 0·2, 0·03

3 **ones** + 8 **tenths** + 6 **hundredths** = 3·86
3 + 0·8 + 0·06 = 3·86

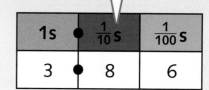

7 **ones** + 5 **tenths** + 2 **hundredths** = 7·52
7 + 0·5 + 0·02 = 7·52

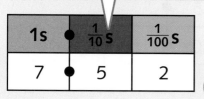

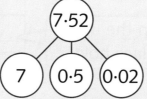

7·52 = 7, 0·5, 0·02

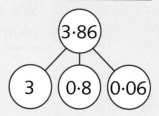

3·86 = 3, 0·8, 0·06

How else could you **partition** (or **regroup**) each of these decimals?

We can position hundredths on a number line and count on and back in hundredths.

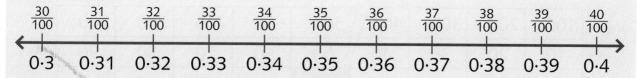

| $\frac{30}{100}$ | $\frac{31}{100}$ | $\frac{32}{100}$ | $\frac{33}{100}$ | $\frac{34}{100}$ | $\frac{35}{100}$ | $\frac{36}{100}$ | $\frac{37}{100}$ | $\frac{38}{100}$ | $\frac{39}{100}$ | $\frac{40}{100}$ |
| 0·3 | 0·31 | 0·32 | 0·33 | 0·34 | 0·35 | 0·36 | 0·37 | 0·38 | 0·39 | 0·4 |

Draw Draw a place value grid, place value counters or a part-whole model to represent each of these decimals.

0·27   4·95

Write For each decimal, what is the value of each of its digits?

10·81   6·03

Pages 72–77

Divide 1- and 2-digit numbers by 10

Pages 44-45, 66-67

When dividing a number by 10, it's important to understand what happens to the place value of its digits.

When we **divide** a 1-digit number by 10, the **value** of the **ones** digit becomes **10 times smaller** and the **digit** moves one **place value** to the right. We include a zero in the **ones** place to act as a **place holder**.

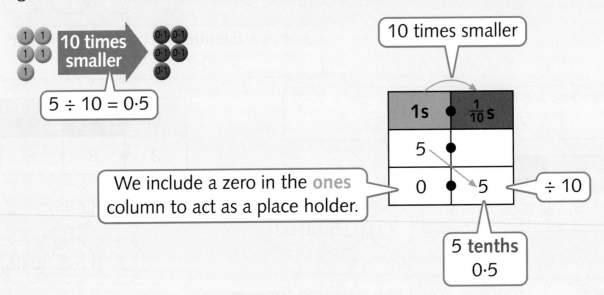

1	1	**10 times smaller** →	0·1	0·1

$5 \div 10 = 0{\cdot}5$

10 times smaller

1s		$\frac{1}{10}$s
5	•	
0	•	5

$\div 10$

We include a zero in the **ones** column to act as a place holder.

5 tenths
0·5

When you move down one row on a Gattegno chart, the number becomes 10 times smaller.

100	200	300	400	500	600	700	800	900
10	20	30	40	50	60	70	80	90
1	2	3	4	5	6	7	8	9
0·1	0·2	0·3	0·4	0·5	0·6	0·7	0·8	0·9

$5 \div 10 = 0{\cdot}5$

When we divide a 2-digit number by 10, the value of each of its digits becomes 10 times smaller and the digits move one place value to the right.

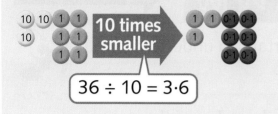

36 ÷ 10 = 3·6

10 times smaller   10 times smaller

10s	1s	•	$\frac{1}{10}$s
3	6	•	
	3	•	6

÷ 10

3 ones
3

6 tenths
0·6

When you move down one row on a Gattegno chart, the number becomes 10 times smaller.

100	200	300	400	500	600	700	800	900
10	20	30	40	50	60	70	80	90
1	2	3	4	5	6	7	8	9
0·1	0·2	0·3	0·4	0·5	0·6	0·7	0·8	0·9

36 ÷ 10 = 3·6

 Draw   Write   Use place value counters, a place value chart or a Gattegno chart to show what happens to the digits when you divide each of these numbers by 10.

9 ÷ 10 = ☐   54 ÷ 10 = ☐

7 ÷ 10 = ☐   81 ÷ 10 = ☐

Pages 72-73

Divide 1- and 2-digit numbers by 100

Pages 44-45, 68-71

When dividing a number by 100, it's important to understand what happens to the place value of its digits.

When we **divide** a 1-digit number by 100, the **value** of the **ones** digit becomes **100 times smaller** and the **digit** moves two **place values** to the right. We include a zero in the **ones** and **tenths** places to act as **place holders**.

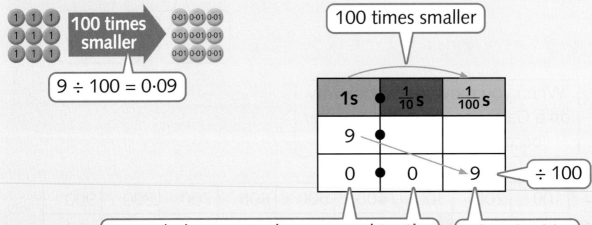

100 times smaller

$9 \div 100 = 0.09$

100 times smaller

1s	$\frac{1}{10}$s	$\frac{1}{100}$s
9		
0	0	9

÷ 100

We include zeros in the **ones** and **tenths** columns to act as place holders.

9 hundredths
0·09

When you move down two rows on a Gattegno chart, the number becomes 100 times smaller.

100	200	300	400	500	600	700	800	900
10	20	30	40	50	60	70	80	90
1	2	3	4	5	6	7	8	9
0·1	0·2	0·3	0·4	0·5	0·6	0·7	0·8	0·9
0·01	0·02	0·03	0·04	0·05	0·06	0·07	0·08	0·09

$9 \div 100 = 0.09$

When we divide a 2-digit number by 100, the value of each of its digits becomes 100 times smaller and the digits move two place values to the right. We include a zero in the ones place to act as a place holder.

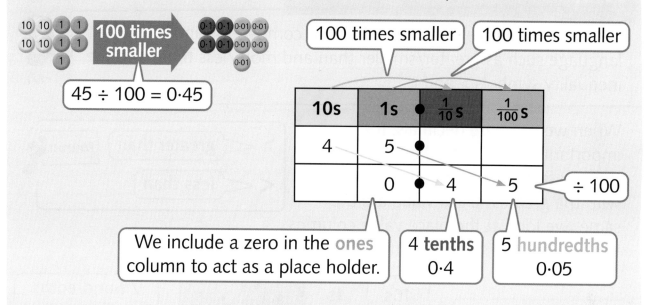

$45 \div 100 = 0.45$

	100 times smaller	100 times smaller

10s	1s •	$\frac{1}{10}$ s	$\frac{1}{100}$ s
4	5 •		
	0 •	4	5

÷ 100

We include a zero in the ones column to act as a place holder.

4 tenths
0.4

5 hundredths
0.05

When you move down two rows on a Gattegno chart, the number becomes 100 times smaller.

100	200	300	400	500	600	700	800	900
10	20	30	40	50	60	70	80	90
1	2	3	4	5	6	7	8	9
0.1	0.2	0.3	0.4	0.5	0.6	0.7	0.8	0.9
0.01	0.02	0.03	0.04	0.05	0.06	0.07	0.08	0.09

$45 \div 100 = 0.45$

 Draw   Write Use place value counters, a place value chart or a Gattegno chart to show what happens to the digits when you divide each of these numbers by 100.

$7 \div 100 = \boxed{}$ $62 \div 100 = \boxed{}$

$3 \div 100 = \boxed{}$ $29 \div 100 = \boxed{}$

Compare and order decimals

Pages 14-17, 66-69

Just like with whole numbers, when we compare decimals we use language such as greater/smaller than and more/less than, and the inequality symbols > and <.

When we **compare** decimals, it's important to start with the **digits** with the greatest **place value**. If the digits with the greatest place value are the same, we look at the place value columns to the right until they are different digits.

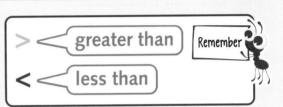

> — greater than   Remember

< — less than

10s	1s	•	$\frac{1}{10}$ s	$\frac{1}{100}$ s
2	8	•	3	7

2 tens has the greatest place value.

7 hundredths has the smallest place value.

Look at each pair of decimals below.

To compare the decimals, look at the digits in place value columns from left to right.

- Start by comparing the **whole numbers**.
- If the whole numbers are the same, compare the **values** of the digits in the **tenths** place.
- If the **tenths** are the same, compare the values of the digits in the hundredths place.

8 tenths are greater than **5 tenths**.

23·85 is greater than 23·51
23·85 > 23·51

10s	1s	•	$\frac{1}{10}$ s
1	6	•	7
1	6	•	9

7 tenths are less than **9 tenths**.

10s	1s	•	$\frac{1}{10}$ s	$\frac{1}{100}$ s
2	3	•	8	5
2	3	•	5	1

16·7 is less than 16·9
16·7 < 16·9

10s	1s	•	$\frac{1}{10}$ s	$\frac{1}{100}$ s
3	5	•	6	7
3	5	•	6	9

7 hundredths are less than **9 hundredths**.

35·67 is less than 35·69
35·67 < 35·69

We can **order** groups of objects or a set of numbers:

in **ascending order** – from **smallest** to **largest/greatest**

or in **descending order** – from largest/greatest to smallest.

Like when we compare decimals, when we order decimals, we start with the digits with the greatest place value. If the digits with the greatest place value are the same, we look at the place value columns to the right until they are different digits.

Descending order – largest to smallest

> If the whole numbers are the same, compare the values of the digits in the **tenths** place.

> Start by comparing whole numbers.

> If the **tenths** are the same, compare the values of the digits in the **hundredths** place.

10s	1s	$\frac{1}{10}$ s	$\frac{1}{100}$ s
	8	5	3
1	1	9	2
1	6	1	4
	8	7	5
1	6	1	7

16·17 > 16·14 > 11·92 > 8·75 > 8·53

Ascending order – smallest to largest

| 23·7 | < | 24·3 | < | 24·8 | < | 25·7 | < | 25·9 |

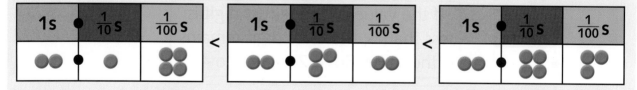

Place each set of decimals in descending order.

4·5 2·3 4·7

4·9 5·2

12·54 11·85 12·45

11·58 12·07

Round decimals

Pages 18–19, 66–69

Rounding means changing a number to another number that is close to it in value. Rounding numbers often makes them easier to use. We round decimals in the same way as we round whole numbers.

Look at these two decimals. **4·2** **4·8**

We **round** decimals to the nearest **whole number**, depending on which whole number the decimal is closer to.

A number line is a useful tool to help with rounding.

4·2 is closer to 4 than to 5. So, the whole number **stays the same**: 4.

4·8 is closer to 5 than to 4. So, **round up** the whole number to 5.

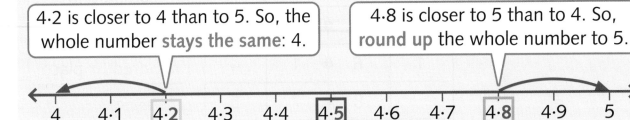

Look at the number 4·5. It's exactly halfway between 4 and 5. The rule for rounding a number with 5 **tenths** is to round up the whole number.

To round decimals to the nearest whole number, look at the **digit** in the **tenths place value** to decide whether the whole number stays the same or rounds up to the next whole number.

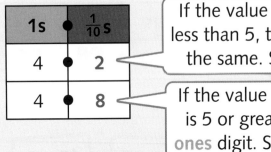

If the value of the **tenths** digit is less than 5, the **ones** digit remains the same. So, 4·2 rounds to 4.

If the value of the **tenths** digit is 5 or greater, round up the **ones** digit. So, 4·8 rounds to 5.

Look at these two decimals. 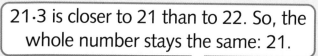 **21·3** **21·7**

How are they the same as the two decimals at the top of page 76?

How are they different?

> 21·3 is closer to 21 than to 22. So, the whole number stays the same: 21.

> 21·7 is closer to 22 than to 21. So, round up the whole number to 22.

| 21 | 21·1 | 21·2 | 21·3 | 21·4 | 21·5 | 21·6 | 21·7 | 21·8 | 21·9 | 22 |

> Look at the number 21·5. It's exactly halfway between 21 and 22. The rule for rounding a number with 5 **tenths** is to round up the whole number.

10s	1s	$\frac{1}{10}$s
2	1	3
2	1	7

> The value of the **tenths** digit is less than 5. So, the ones digit remains the same. 21·3 rounds to 21.

> The value of the **tenths** digit is 5 or greater. So, round up the ones digit. 21·7 rounds to 22.

 Write Round each of these decimals to the nearest whole number.

10·6 **3·1** **42·5** **13·9** **87·4** **60·2**

Consider:

- which whole numbers the decimal lies between
- which place value column you need to focus on when rounding to the nearest whole number
- whether the decimal rounds up or does not round up.

 Draw Choose one decimal number from the cards above and draw a number line to show how you rounded the decimal to the nearest whole number.

Year 4 Number facts

Multiples of 100 addition and subtraction facts

If you know that 6 + 8 = 14, you can use this to work out facts such as:

600 + 800 = 1,400

Addition can be done in any order.

So, 600 + 800 = 1,400 and 800 + 600 = 1,400

Addition is the inverse of subtraction.

So, if you know that 600 + 800 = 1,400

you also know that

1,400 − 600 = 800 and 1,400 − 800 = 600

+	0	100	200	300	400	500	600	700	800	900	1,000
0	0	100	200	300	400	500	600	700	800	900	1,000
100	100	200	300	400	500	600	700	800	900	1,000	1,100
200	200	300	400	500	600	700	800	900	1,000	1,100	1,200
300	300	400	500	600	700	800	900	1,000	1,100	1,200	1,300
400	400	500	600	700	800	900	1,000	1,100	1,200	1,300	1,400
500	500	600	700	800	900	1,000	1,100	1,200	1,300	1,400	1,500
600	600	700	800	900	1,000	1,100	1,200	1,300	1,400	1,500	1,600
700	700	800	900	1,000	1,100	1,200	1,300	1,400	1,500	1,600	1,700
800	800	900	1,000	1,100	1,200	1,300	1,400	1,500	1,600	1,700	1,800
900	900	1,000	1,100	1,200	1,300	1,400	1,500	1,600	1,700	1,800	1,900
1,000	1,000	1,100	1,200	1,300	1,400	1,500	1,600	1,700	1,800	1,900	2,000

Multiplication and division facts

Multiplication can be done in any order.

So, 3 × 4 = 12 and 4 × 3 = 12

Multiplication is the inverse of division.

So, if you know that 3 × 4 = 12 you also know that

12 ÷ 4 = 3 and 12 ÷ 3 = 4

×	1	2	3	4	5	6	7	8	9	10	11	12
1	1	2	3	4	5	6	7	8	9	10	11	12
2	2	4	6	8	10	12	14	16	18	20	22	24
3	3	6	9	12	15	18	21	24	27	30	33	36
4	4	8	12	16	20	24	28	32	36	40	44	48
5	5	10	15	20	25	30	35	40	45	50	55	60
6	6	12	18	24	30	36	42	48	54	60	66	72
7	7	14	21	28	35	42	49	56	63	70	77	84
8	8	16	24	32	40	48	56	64	72	80	88	96
9	9	18	27	36	45	54	63	72	81	90	99	108
10	10	20	30	40	50	60	70	80	90	100	110	120
11	11	22	33	44	55	66	77	88	99	110	121	132
12	12	24	36	48	60	72	84	96	108	120	132	144

Multiples of 10 multiplication and division facts

If you know that
$3 \times 4 = 12$, you can use this to
work out facts such as:

$30 \times 4 = 120$ and $3 \times 40 = 120$

Multiplication is the inverse of
division. So, if you know that
$30 \times 4 = 120$

you also know that

$120 \div 4 = 30$ and $120 \div 30 = 4$

×	10	20	30	40	50	60	70	80	90	100	110	120
1	10	20	30	40	50	60	70	80	90	100	110	120
2	20	40	60	80	100	120	140	160	180	200	220	240
3	30	60	90	120	150	180	210	240	270	300	330	360
4	40	80	120	160	200	240	280	320	360	400	440	480
5	50	100	150	200	250	300	350	400	450	500	550	600
6	60	120	180	240	300	360	420	480	540	600	660	720
7	70	140	210	280	350	420	490	560	630	700	770	840
8	80	160	240	320	400	480	560	640	720	800	880	960
9	90	180	270	360	450	540	630	720	810	900	990	1,080
10	100	200	300	400	500	600	700	800	900	1,000	1,100	1,200
11	110	220	330	440	550	660	770	880	990	1,100	1,210	1,320
12	120	240	360	480	600	720	840	960	1,080	1,200	1,320	1,440

If you know that $3 \times 4 = 12$ and $30 \times 4 = 120$, you can use this to work
out facts such as:

$300 \times 4 = 1,200$ and $3 \times 400 = 1,200$

$1,200 \div 4 = 300$ and $1,200 \div 300 = 4$